Contents

List of tables in text

List of figures in text

List of tables in Appendix

FOREWORD

The recording of morbidity and mortality data has been fundamental to our study of disease and has helped us to understand the origins of morbid processes. The first comprehensive attempt to accomplish a national recording of morbidity in Ireland was devised by Sir William Wilde for the first Irish census of population in 1841. Not very much progress was made during the ensuing century, so that even as late as the 1940s a substantial proportion of deaths in people aged over 60 were certified as being due to from 'senility' and death statistics did not record the site of cancers causing death.

Progress in what is now called information technology remained slow, both in relation to disease and death recording, and it is only in recent years that a national cancer registry has been introduced. Information on health service activity still remains limited and the system monitoring general hospital activity, the Hospital In-Patient Enquiry (HIPE) introduced in the 1970s, does not cover the private sector. Patient management systems, too, are still in their infancy. In addition, there is not in Ireland a personal identifier given at birth, which, if it existed, would enable the health (or disease) status of cohorts of individuals to be tracked, with obvious advantage for our understanding of scientific and clinical issues and for the rational planning of health services. Reports examining the Irish health care system have repeatedly complained that their efforts have been thwarted by data deficiencies. These deficits also encompass budgetary and expenditure data.

As matters stand, Ireland's spend on information technology in health is at a lower level than that of most other developed countries. Slowly, these deficiencies are being recognised and there is growing support for the collection of quality data to inform the development of health services. In association with publication of the health strategy document, *Quality and Fairness: A Health System for You* (Department of Health and Children, 2001), a separate publication *National Health Information Strategy* (Department of Health and Children, 2004) has now also been published.

In the field of mental illness, it is true to say that the information base was established earlier and more completely in both the nineteenth and twentieth centuries than in any other health field. In 1846 the establishment of the Inspectorate of Lunacy with the statutory obligation of reporting to the Lord Lieutenant on the state of asylums annually led to detailed reports on admitted and resident patients and other matters. These were continued for the 26 counties, by successive Inspectors of Mental Hospitals, following the foundation of the State. With the setting up of the Medico-Social Research Board (MRSB), later to become the Health Research Board (HRB), the National Psychiatric In-patient Reporting System (NPIRS) was inaugurated in 1971. Prior to this, however, the Department of Health, at the instigation of the Commission of Enquiry on Mental Illness (Department of Health, 1966), had carried out a census of patients resident in mental hospitals and thereafter instigated an individualised system of recording admissions and discharges, both later to be analysed and published by the MRSB. These nineteenth and twentieth century sources supply the data on which this publication is based.

One of the most remarkable phenomena of health care of the past two centuries has been the revolution in policy in providing care for the mentally ill. The nineteenth and early twentieth century governments and administrators embarked on a policy of institutionalising such persons in asylums specifically designed and built for that purpose. The policy was clear and unambiguous and was pursued relentlessly by central and local powers and its progress was recorded year by year by the Reports of the Inspectors based at the Office of Lunacy at Dublin Castle. New asylums were built and existing ones enlarged and by 1900 the task was almost complete, although it staggered on to its culmination during the first half of the twentieth century, losing the fervour of the earlier century, until finally trickling to a halt about 1960.

And then the scene changed, somersaulted, even, as if the old order had exhausted itself and was seeking newer sources of inspiration. The numbers institutionalised began to fall. In truth, no one knew why. And then, as if following nature, policy acquiesced and the new philosophy was articulated in the 1966 *Report of the Commission on Mental Illness* (Department of Health, 1966) and re-affirmed in the later policy document *Planning for the Future* (Department of Health, 1984). Henceforth, the commitment was to de-institutionalisation, turning the nineteenth century on its head.

It is the purpose of this document to chart the rise and fall of these changes in mental health care from historical sources, briefly during the epoch of increase, and in more detail during the period of decline from Department of Health returns from 1963 to 1970, from then onwards from NPIRS and other data sources. Chapter One charts the rise of the institutionalisation of the mentally ill from the mid-1700s up to 1900. Chapter Two details the continuing rise of institutionalisation up to 1960. Chapter Three surveys admissions and discharges from 1960 and describes the establishment of the National Psychiatric In-patient Reporting as the vehicle for this. Chapter Four describes the decline in institutionalisation and Chapter Five attempts to place these changes in a setting of social concern stressing the link between deprivation and mental illness already well established in the early nineteenth century, as exemplified by the pervading preoccupation with the 'lunatic poor' and the more general but overlapping provision for the deprived by the workhouse system of relief, and in the twentieth century by the distinctions between private and public care. Data used for the twenty-first century are those most recent for the parameter under consideration, in some cases, 2001, and in others, 2002.

Finally, in the wider context of rational provision of services for the mentally ill in the new millennium, and in light of newer, more sophisticated information technology in the health care field, some suggestions and pleas are made for the resources to fill the gaps in our knowledge of the extent of morbidity, the effectiveness, efficacy and utility of current services and treatments and, more importantly, what will be required to meet this need in the future in the important, but often neglected, field of mental illness.

CHAPTER 1

CHAPTER 1

The Great Confinement
up to 1900

The Eighteenth century and before

Before the eighteenth century, organised response to the problem of major psychiatric illness in Ireland or elsewhere was limited. However, major changes in the demography of European populations were to have substantial consequences for societal attitudes to the mentally ill. During the century, the Irish population increased until by 1800 it stood at an estimated eight million. This great increase was due to increased life expectation and falling mortality from the common infectious diseases such as cholera, typhus, smallpox and tuberculosis, because of improved nutrition. It is reasonable to suggest that before this improvement the life expectation of the mentally ill, once they had become ill, and of the mentally handicapped may have been at considerable disadvantage compared to the mentally healthy. With improved survival however, these groups may have become a more visible element of society. Although this speculation cannot be satisfactorily resolved because of the lack of appropriate demographic and other data before 1800, it is worth bearing in mind that, as far as the intellectually disabled are concerned, an analogous situation has become evident in the late twentieth century. The substantial increase in life expectation of the mentally handicapped has resulted in increased community burden because the increased prevalence of the condition due to increased survival has outstripped the provision of residential places (Health Research Board, 2003).

The eighteenth century response in Ireland to those mentally ill was sporadic and unco-ordinated. Dean Swift, with some satire, in 1745 bequeathed a legacy to establish St Patrick's Hospital in Dublin to care for fee-paying and pauper inmates. In Cork, in 1799, a further private hospital, Citadella, was opened by Dr William Saunders Hallaran, who could be called the first Irish psychiatrist (to use modern terminology) because of his writings on the subject of insanity and his concern for the insane, even if this led to such treatments as the notorious Hallaran's Swing. Meanwhile, the social problems caused by beggars and the indigent poor had grown, or had been perceived to have done so, to such an extent that campaigns mounted by such as Dean Woodworth of Clogher led to legislation in 1772 setting up Houses of Industry at Dublin, Clonmel, Cork, Waterford and Limerick. The dual purpose of these Houses was to confine and control 'sturdy beggars and vagabonds' and to give some shelter to the 'deserving poor'. Inevitably the numbers of lunatics among those admitted grew to the extent that special cells were provided for them. The Prisons Act of 1787 gave powers for the establishment of lunatic wards in the Houses of Industry; in the event only four, Dublin, Cork, Waterford and Limerick provided such wards, which were then subject to inspection and report by the Inspectors General of Prisons. The Dublin House of Industry in time evolved into what was later to become St Laurence's Hospital and the Richmond Lunatic Asylum. In the Cork House of Industry, Hallaran was appointed to take charge of the lunatic ward. These initiatives apart, no specific or general response was made during the century to the problem of the lunatic poor.

The Nineteenth Century

By the turn of the century the emerging social conscience, responding to the ever-more-visible problems of the new society, searched for solutions that were as comforting as they were useful. And as Finnane (1981) put it 'Confronted with the evidence of social disorder, overpopulation and an ailing economy, reforming politicians, political economists and social observers, rising professionals, philantropists and humanitarians of various persuasions and motivations all sought to bring order to Ireland' – including order to the problems created by mental disorder.

Matters were little different in the neighbouring island. Jones (1960), speaking of England, recorded: 'In the first half of the nineteenth century, the tide of industrial change brought new wealth and new opportunities to a few, but squalor and hardship to many. The social problems with which many small rural communities had dealt casually, but on the whole effectively, became acute in the towns, where families crowded together in conditions of dirt and disease and despair: but industrialisation, if it intensified social distress, also provided the means of dealing with it. The very force of distress provided a new social conscience, a desire to tackle the age-old problems of poverty and sickness.' The problems were similar elsewhere in Europe and Foucault (1989) described 'the great confinement', as he called it, in France, detailing the confinement of mad people in prisons and elsewhere and the administrative responses to the problem as it grew and became more visible.

In Ireland, whereas industrialisation may not have been such a relevant factor with the great majority of the population still rural dwellers living at or on below subsistence level on limited agricultural production, the horrors of the potato famines of the first half of the century exercised a notable effect on mortality. The impact on lunacy and the response to it brought about by this cataclysm have yet to be explored. In any event, the perception of the problem and the response to it were contemporaneous in both England and Ireland. Even if the perception of the social and other difficulties posed by lunacy became starkly apparent only after the Act of Union, there are good grounds to believe that the Irish response, although slowly unfolding, was more thorough and earlier completed than that of England – that is if the rate of progress and completion of the policy common to both jurisdictions, institutionalisation, was to be the yardstick, although it could be argued that this was the more easily accomplished in a country with a falling population (Ireland) than in one where it was growing rapidly (England).

The bringing of social order involved the establishment of new social systems, including those for the containment of the lunatic poor. Whether this movement was also driven by a real increase in the incidence of major mental illness around 1800, brought about by forces other than social change, as some have suggested, remains an open question. In any event, as far as Ireland was concerned, the ultimate result was a national lunatic asylum system that was the envy of many other jurisdictions. The motivation for this concern and the response to it were as much humanitarian as they were utilitarian – to house and care for – even if the aspiration to cure was largely unfulfilled.

In 1804 a House of Commons Select Committee recommended the building of four provincial asylums in Ireland, including one in Dublin, each to have 250 beds. The response was limited to the building of one asylum only, the new Richmond, replacing the lunatic ward in the Dublin House of Industry and on a site adjacent to it, between 1810 and 1815, to the designs of Francis Johnston, an architect of many respected public and private commissions. Acts of 1817 and 1821 providing for the setting up of asylums for the lunatic poor in Ireland gave official recognition of the extent of the problem, and thus the need to respond to it on a specialty basis was established. The philosophy underlying policy has been spelt out by Jones (1960). Insanity 'is quite different from physical illness, and quite unlike normal behaviour. It is generally caused by poor heredity, or by drink, or possibly by starvation. Insane people should be sent to asylums, and most of them will have to stay there for life. Special authorities should be set up for the running of asylums, under a strong central control. Patients have to be treated under compulsion and they must be locked in, in case they try to escape. The only way in which they can be detained without infringing the liberty of the subject is to delay certification until the patient is obviously, and perhaps incurably, insane. Early treatment might mean wrongful detention in some cases, and our first duty is to protect the sane.' Not all observers of this practise of regulation were approving and some concurred with Dostoievsky (quoted by Foucault 1989) commenting that 'it is not by confining one's neighbour that one is convinced of one's own sanity'.

The legislation of 1817 and 1821 was enabling only; it did not oblige local bodies to provide asylums and, more importantly, did not allocate funds for building them, although later enactments did so, at least to a limited extent. Consequently, there was no great rush to put stones and mortar together and in the earlier part of the nineteenth century provision of asylums was slow. By 1831 only five had been constructed, Armagh, Belfast, Derry, Limerick and Richmond (Dublin). Collectively they catered for 791 inmates. These original four and the later parts of the Richmond were built by the Board of Works at the instigation of the Commissioners for the Erection of Lunatic Asylums. Established under an Act of 1817, they appointed the well-known architect Francis Johnston and his cousin William Murray to design them to a common formula, two storey and classical. The next decade saw the addition of Ballinasloe, Carlow, Clonmel, Maryborough (Portlaoise) and Waterford and the extension of the Richmond, adding another 414 places and bringing the total to 1,205. All these were part of the first wave of asylum building and all conformed to the Johnston/Murray architectural formula, although Johnston had died in 1829. In 1835, responsibility for the building of asylums passed exclusively to the Board of Works.

Perhaps because of the pre-occupation with the programme of workhouse construction, no new asylums were built in the early 1840s. However, legislation in 1845 provided for two new asylums – a criminal one in Dundrum, Dublin, and a 500-bed asylum in Cork, designed by a local architect and opened in 1850. This latter, the Eglington Asylum, was originally in three separate blocks, later to be joined together, in the interest of providing more accommodation, to become the longest façade of any building in the country. In the following decade and largely in the face of demands for more accommodation coming from, among others, the Inspectorate of Lunacy, and because there was still reckoned to be a substantial number of lunatics 'at large', construction resumed, with the Board of Works commissioning individual architects to design the second wave of asylum building, mainly of somewhat grim, three-storey gothic revival structures, of which the prototype was Mulvany's Mullingar asylum. While the issue of whether to enlarge existing asylums or build new ones, as a policy of decentralisation and of assuaging local political interest, was being debated, a Board of Control was established in 1859, comprising two Commissioners of Public Works and two Inspectors of Lunacy. The following year, George Wilkinson, who, in the face of local opposition (he had come from England), had been responsible for the design of the workhouses, was appointed architect to the Board of Control. Local authorities were given the option of employing their own architects or employing Wilkinson. Two authorities employed him, resulting in the rather similar asylums in Letterkenny and Castlebar.

As the century progressed, the issue whether the accommodation provided was adequate became central to answering the question whether more asylums were needed and whether existing ones should be enlarged. To answer it, the good offices of the Royal Irish Constabulary were invoked to estimate the numbers of lunatics still at large and in need of asylum. This was carried out by divisional constabulary conducting censuses in their own districts – the one and only time in which a community prevalence study of mental illness was carried out in this country.

The other nineteenth century asylums of the third phase were planned and designed by individual architects, often working with local surveyors. Of interest was that the Monaghan asylum, designed by McCurdy, was the first in the country to break away from the continuous corridor model and adopt a pavilion or villa format (O'Dwyer, 1997) This final phase of building resulted in such beguiling outcomes as the Florentine palazzo building at Ennis (1868) and culminated in the 1890s in the building of the auxiliary asylum to the Richmond at Portrane, Co Dublin, the largest capital project ever undertaken by the colonial administration in Ireland. Of course, as well as new building there had been considerable additions to existing structures. By 1900 the job had been done – the policy of housing the lunatic poor articulated almost a century earlier had been accomplished – and 21,000 citizens, 0.5% of the population of the 32 counties, was now housed in the district asylums, with the exception of a small number who remained in workhouses.

The history of institutionalisation of the mentally ill in England ran a rather similar course as documented by Jones (1955). Spurred by the same considerations as those in Ireland, and particularly by rising industrialisation, concern at conditions in private madhouses and the growing appreciation of mental illness as a palpable reality because of the mental incapacity of George III (later to be attributed to physical causes, McAlpine, 1992), the early nineteenth century saw the setting up of a Select Committee in 1807 whose report led to the County Asylum Act of 1808 and a further Select Committee of 1815. The result was that by 1842 there were 3,743 residents in 17 county asylums in England. This provision was to continue to increase until well into the twentieth century, before beginning to decline in 1955. The problem and the response to it was very similar in other Western European countries: in Italy, for example there were, by 1866, 27 public asylums, five private and four wards in general hospitals for mentally ill persons (Tagliavini, 1985). In the United States, whereas in 1820 there were fewer than 10 mental hospitals, by the outbreak of the Civil War (1861) there was one or more in every state (Grob, 1971).

An Act of 1826, in Ireland, gave power to the Inspectors General of Prisons to visit and inspect madhouses and places where idiots and lunatics were confined and to report on such visits to grand juries. In 1842, by enactment, the Inspectors General of Prisons became Inspectors of Lunatic Asylums. Across the water, in England, and in the same year, an Act established the Metropolitan Commissioners in Lunacy, requiring them to inspect every house licensed for the reception of insane persons, to inspect every part of the premises and to see every confined patient and exercise other responsibilities on inspection very similar to those required of the Inspectors of Mental Hospitals as set up by legislation in Ireland, over a century later, in 1945. The Commissioners published the first report of their inspections, the Lunacy Report in 1844.

Back in Ireland on the first of January 1846, an independent Inspectorate of Lunacy was established and the first Inspector took up post, to be followed by a second the following year. The Inspectorate, from this point on, submitted annual reports to the Lords Lieutenants and Governors General of Ireland on the state of the lunatic asylums and their inmates. Because of the wealth of detail contained in these yearly reports, they must be regarded as the first reporting system in the mental health services of this country. Details were given, not alone of the numbers resident, but also of those admitted, discharged, dying in, and escaping from, lunatic asylums but also on lunatics in union workhouses and in private asylums. Information was also supplied on the asylum workforce in numbers, wages etc. and on the number of beds in dormitories and on the disposition of rooms in each asylum. The dietary and details of the cultivation and production of asylum farms were also included. In the later nineteenth century diagnostic details on the condition affecting every admission and resident were also supplied, including the supposed cause of the condition. In 1905 the Inspectors were given responsibility for inspecting those Inebriate Retreats and Reformatories set up under the Inebriates Act of 1898 at Ennis, Wexford and Waterford, but which, never being very successful, were to close within a few years. By the twentieth century the Inspectors of Asylums had become Inspectors of Mental Hospitals but by mid-century their reports had become less detailed and informative as reporting systems, although this situation had been redressed towards the century's end.

Not everyone was happy about conditions in the eighteenth century asylums and, in particular, a report of the Commission of Enquiry on the State of Lunatic Asylums in Ireland, which was published in 1858, found much to criticise in the conditions and the administration of these institutions. Not least, it questioned the presence of the Inspectors as ex-officio members of the boards of governors of the very asylums they were expected to inspect. Stung by these strictures the Inspector of the day, Dr Nugent, riposted in 'Observations on the Report of the Commissioners of Inquiry into Lunatic Asylums (Ireland) in a Letter to the Right Honourable Lord Viscount Naas, M.P., Chief Secretary' attempting to refute the extensive criticisms made by the Commissioners, two of whom, being English, 'could have no personal knowledge of proceedings at this side of the water' particularly after 'a cursory visit of five or six weeks'. In defence of the Irish asylums Nugent claimed 'they were eminently successful as curative establishments ...... placing them on an equality with any similar establishments in Europe - superior, perhaps, to most.' He also extolled their merits in being free from abuse and referred to the 'wondrous immunity of them from accidents and deeds of violence, considering the excitability of our race'.

There was much puzzlement in official and scientific quarters as to the reason why the lunatic population was still increasing at a time when both the prison and workhouse numbers were falling (there are those who claim that in the late twentieth century, with increased psychiatric de-institutionalisation, this process has reversed itself – and whereas there are now grounds for believing that some seriously mentally ill persons are in prisons who should be more appropriately dealt with by psychiatric services, there are no data to indicate whether this proportion has grown pari passu with psychiatric de-institutilisation other than that the prison population as a whole has grown). In response, an investigation was set up and led to the publication of a Special Report from the Inspectors of Lunatics *On the Alleged Increasing Prevalence of Insanity in Ireland* (Special Report from the Inspectors of Lunacy to the Chief Secretary, 1894).

The investigation of this question was bedevilled by two important matters. The first of these was that the nineteenth century lunacy system catered for two groups, lunatics, and also idiots, or what today are called the intellectually disabled. The second problem was that the location of lunatics, for ascertainment or counting purposes, was in three different places, or, if as was the case in the earlier part of the century, in prisons as well, four. By the 1870s there were no lunatics recorded as being in prisons. The other locations were the lunatic asylums, where policy dictated that all of them should be, and where indeed as the century progressed they were increasingly to be found; the workhouses; and 'at large' or to use today's terminology, in the community, but with what measure of support, familial or other, we do not know. However, since figures were available for all of these locations the matter was less of a problem than it appeared. As lunatics were transferred from workhouses to asylums another problem arose and that was, that in attempting to derive first admission rates to asylums and to use them as measures of incidence, or in nineteenth century parlance, rates of 'occurring' lunacy, the figures available did not always distinguish between first admissions of a lunatic to any establishment and transfers of those already in workhouses or, in the earlier part of the century, from prisons as well.

One suspects that the differentiation between lunatics and idiots was not that sound as evidenced by the fact that, whereas in 1851 the number of idiots ascertained, wherever located, was almost equal to the number of lunatics – 4,905 as against 5,074 lunatics – by 1891, not alone had the total of both groups more than doubled to 21,188, but the balance had shifted towards lunatics – 14,945 as against 6,243 idiots. In other words, while both had increased, the increase was much greater for lunacy. Of interest, too, was the fact that, whereas by 1871 there were virtually none of either group remaining in prisons, the number of lunatics in workhouses continued to increase, from 494 in 1851 to 2,787 in 1891, while the number of idiots in this location remained steady, 1,129 in 1851 and 1,170 in 1891. Over the same 40 years the number of idiots in asylums increased from 202 to 996. Despite the growth of institutional care for both groups, the numbers at large did not fall greatly. In 1851 there were 1,073 lunatics and 3,562 idiots in this category, compared to 893 and 4,077 respectively in 1891. The greater numbers of idiots at large may have reflected greater social tolerance of this group.

Table 1.1   Number of lunatics and idiots at large, in asylums, in prisons and in workhouses 1851, 1861, 1871, 1881 and 1891.

	Lunatics					Idiots					Total lunatics and idiots
	At large	In asylums	In prisons	In workhouses	Total	At Large	In Asylums	In Prisons	In Workhouses	Total	
1851	1,073	3,234	273	494	5,074	3,562	202	13	1,129	4,906	9,980
1861	1,602	4,613	273	577	7,065	5,675	403	21	934	7,033	14,098
1871	1,343	7,141	5	1,274	9,763	5,147	410	2	1,183	6,742	16,505
1881	943	7,547	0	1,284	9,774	4,548	1,896	0	2,195	8,639	18,413
1891	893	11,265	0	2,787	14,945	4,077	996	0	1,170	6,243	21,188

Source: Special Report from the Inspectors of Lunatics to the Chief Secretary. (1894) *Alleged Increasing Prevalence of Insanity in Ireland.* Dublin: HMSO.

As the table shows, the proportional increase in the two groups was quite unequal, with lunacy almost trebling in the forty years from 1851 to 1891 but idiocy showing a much smaller increase of just over one quarter. There were curious inequalities in increases over the years, with a very large increase in idiocy from 1851 to 1861, followed by a slight fall to 1871, a rise in the next 10 years and then another small decline to 1891. In lunacy, after stabilisation from 1871 to 1881, there was quite a jump to 1891 and, because of virtually no decrease in those at large, only to a limited extent do these changes between groups appear to be compensatory.

What is clear overall is that there appeared to be a substantial increase in lunacy from 1851 to 1891. One wonders whether the doubling of lunatics in workhouse and the halving of idiots from 1881 to 1891 was not a reciprocal artefact. Indeed Drapes (1894), whom we shall meet later, was not unaware of the difficulties of some of these distinctions. Commenting on these changes in the location of idiots he said 'Such abrupt changes in the numbers can hardly, I think, be held to indicate a sudden outbreak of idiocy, or an equally sudden extinction of a large mass of existing idiocy, but rather an uncertainty in the application of the term idiot on the part of those who made the returns.'

It is instructive to compare the comparative efficiency with which Ireland on the one hand and England on the other provided asylum places to identified lunatics. In Ireland in 1861 out of a total of 7065 known, 4613 or 65% were in asylums (Table 1.1), compared to less than half of 44,695 in England in 1864 (Walton, 1983). In both jurisdictions, sizeable numbers remained in workhouses.

Instructed by the Chief Secretary to investigate the 'difficult and vexed' question of the alleged increase in the prevalence of insanity in Ireland as apparently evidenced by the increasing demand for asylum places and the almost immediate filling of these places as soon as they became available, the Special Report set out the conclusions 'at which the best sources of information which have been open to us to arrive (sic)'.

These sources were in fact the medical superintendents of the district asylums who were circularised by the Inspectors in December 1893. The circular letter requested information relating to the 10 years ending on the 31 December 1892 on the superintendents general impressions of the matter, an accurate return of first admissions, including the duration of mental disease on admission, a return of workhouses cases, distinguishing first admissions, and giving, where possible, the duration of mental disease on admission, the number of deaths and the average mortality 'in your asylum' during the 10 years, and the causes of insanity in patients admitted. In addition, the superintendents were asked for any particular observations that they might have on the question of causation by heredity, the influence exercised in this respect by either the abuse of alcohol or any changes in the habits or dietary of the people. In addition, the effects of emigration on the numbers of the insane were to be noted. 'Emigration having been represented to be, in its indirect effects, largely accountable for the increased number of admissions to the asylums in recent years, it becomes very important to ascertain with precision, how the actual facts stand as to this; and you will probably be able without much difficulty, to say how far in the case of your district, the removal in this way of the wage-earning members of families has been followed by the transfer to the asylum of mentally affected persons previously maintained in their own homes'.

Reports of varying length and perspicacity were submitted by all superintendents, with those from the superintendents of the Richmond, Wexford and Waterford asylums being the most comprehensive. The Inspectors then summarised the contents of the reports and added some interpretations of their own.

The report pointed out that; 'In workhouses the gross total of the accumulation of insanity is shown from year to year, but no means exist of ascertaining the admissions, discharges or deaths.' 'It is admitted that the number of first attacks affords the only reliable basis of accurately calculating the amount of freshly occurring insanity - hence it becomes important to ascertain among first admissions, over a series of years, the duration of the mental disease previous to admission, so as to determine with precision the proportion of first attacks to the general population.'

The Inspectors then state that the number of first admissions has increased 'pari passu' with the total admissions into asylums. Having made this statement about admissions, the report returns to the rate of insane and idiots in the four locations of asylums, workhouses, at large or in prisons and points out that this had gone from 150 per 100,000 population in 1851 to 450 in 1891. Then, returning to the matter of admissions, the report shows an increase from 2,366 in 1880 to 3,181 in 1892 and points out that in this time period the number of removals through discharge, death or escape had not correspondingly gone up, although there had been an increase from 2,189 in 1880 to 2,781 in 1892. 'The number of discharges have [sic] not increased in a like ratio, as it was at one time supposed would have been the case under improved treatment. Again the mortality in Irish asylums has been so low that it has always largely tended to favour [sic] accumulation in these institutions. Practically all the incurable cases have to be retained as permanent patients,' hence the accumulation, the Inspectors added. 'Undoubtedly, the large emigration which has taken from this country within the past fifty years of the strong and healthy has led to an increased and undue proportion of the insane and imbecile, as well as of other defective classes, among our population and the numbers of admissions in recent years are swelled by the return of emigrants who have broken down mentally either from hereditary tendency or, from their inability from other causes to bear the strain of their new condition and surroundings.'

While qualifying any conclusions that they had made on the grounds of 'insufficiency of lunatic statistics' (although they make no suggestions as to how these might be improved), the Inspectors conclude that 'some absolute increase of insanity is taking place in certain districts of this country'. They add that such increase will prove to be comparatively small in amount. More generally, they conclude that 'the great increase of the insane under care is mainly due to accumulation and is, so far, an apparent and not a real increase'. The yearly increase in admissions, they deduce, is drawn from the reserve of unregistered insane as shown by the reduction of numbers at large in successive population censuses, from 1851 to 1891 – in other words by increased asylum accommodation. But this conclusion is not borne out by the facts as the data show only a very small reduction in lunatics at large and an actual increase in idiots in this category over these 40 years. They then speculate on the factors which contributed to the development of occurring insanity and enumerate heredity and consanguineous marriages exemplifying 'certain secluded valleys in the west and south of Ireland where inter-marriage is common'. And they contrast this with the observation of the superintendent of Letterkenny Asylum that insanity was infrequent in the population of Tory Island. They implicate also the 'innutritious' dietary of the poorer population and the misuse of certain nervous stimulants such as alcohol, ether, tea and tobacco.

Some additional points were made by individual superintendents. Thus, Connolly Norman of the Richmond felt that the prejudice against sending patients to the asylum was dying out and people were becoming less tolerant of having persons of unsound mind in their midst. He also pointed out that Poor Law authorities were aware that workhouses were unsuitable for the insane and were increasingly sending them to the asylums, while at the same time refusing to take the recovered insane from asylums. He felt that in his district the increase in insanity was largely confined to the urban population of the City and County of Dublin because of the increasing population there and of the large 'floating element – waifs and strays of all kinds contribute to swell this drift population'. He added that acute mania 'the most curable of forms' was becoming rare, while melancholia and primary mental deterioration and organic brain disease and general paralysis were increasing.

In the *Journal of Mental Science* in October 1894 Thomas Drapes, Resident Medical Superintendent of the District Asylum, Enniscorthy, delivered a paper 'On the Alleged Increase of Insanity in Ireland'. Ireland, he pointed out, 'possesses the unique and unenviable distinction of a continuously increasing amount of insanity with a continuously decreasing population' and he then went on to a thoroughgoing analysis of what statistics were available to him and to comparisons between the Irish and English scenes. He stressed that 'the only true criterion of the increase or decrease of insanity is to be found in the number of first attacks' and 'I think that the large majority of what are entered as first admissions are also cases of first attacks'. He then goes on to examine the first admission figures for Ireland and England. From these he concluded that the ratio of first admissions to population had increased considerably and must 'be regarded as indicating a decided increase in occurring insanity'. He added that the rate of increase was on the decline and that, if removals from workhouses to asylums were excluded from the Irish tables, as they were in the English ones, the ratio of first admissions would be actually lower in Ireland than in England. He concluded that the number of the insane in Ireland was far higher in proportion to the population than it was in England and that the rate of increase had been much more rapid in Ireland.

Further, the rate of total admissions to population had increased steadily, particularly from 1875 to 1885 and, while the rate was lower than in England up to 1881, it then overtook the latter and has increased at a greater rate since then. This appeared to be due to the far higher proportion of re-admissions in Ireland than in England. The recovery rate, he noted, was somewhat higher in Ireland but, on the other hand, the discharge rate of the unrecovered was considerably higher in England. The death rate in Irish asylums was much lower than in English asylums. 'As to the chief cause of the lower death rate in Ireland, this can hardly be a matter of doubt. One disease, and one only, is common in England, rare in Ireland. I allude, of course, to general paralysis' accounting for hardly more than 2% in Ireland as against 18 – 20% in England. 'So that if we were to say that the apparent excess of insanity in Ireland over that of England is due to the absence of general paralysis (general paralysis was a late complication of syphilis), the statement would not be very far from the truth.' After some speculation as to the reason for the difference of the prevalence of the condition between the two jurisctictions he concludes that 'strange as it may appear, the preponderance of apparent insanity in this country may be said to be largely due to the virtue of its inhabitants'.

In summary, Drapes claimed: 'The net result, then, of this examination is to show that, while there is an undoubted increase in occurring insanity, as indicated by the records of first admissions, by far the larger part of the apparent increase in insanity generally is due to accumulation, and that the seeming preponderance of insanity in Ireland, as compared to England, is fictitious, and depends entirely on the greater amount of accumulation in Ireland, occasioned by the lower death-rate in that country, and (possibly) the lower rate of discharge of the unrecovered.'

In the same issue of the *Journal of Mental Science,* D Hack Tuke of the Retreat at York, an asylum founded by the Quakers celebrated for its 'moral' or kind and understanding treatment of the insane, and who commented on Drapes paper, was also examining the question of the alleged increase in insanity as it applied to England and Wales (Tuke, 1894). His conclusions were remarkably similar to those of the Irish Inspectors dealing with their own situation. In short he concluded from the evidence of data available to him that 'the increase in insanity is apparent rather than real, being mainly due to accumulation'. It was his view that this accumulation was age-related and occurred in persons aged over 45, rather than in those under this age, and saw the accumulation due to lower death rate, 'the chronicity of the disease, and the lamentable tendency to relapse'. It will be recalled that the lower death rate (than admission rate) figured also in the Irish considerations.

In relation to occurring insanity, Tuke's conclusions echoed those of the Irish Inspectors and were bedevilled by the same main obstacle in computation – that transfers from workhouses to asylums were not taken into account in computing first admission rates. However that might be, he, too, arrived at the similar conclusion that there had been no real increase in first admission rates and, therefore, of occurring insanity. In relation to residence rates, he pointed out, as further evidence in favour of accumulating rather than occurring insanity, that the increase was in the over 45 years rather than in those younger. As in Ireland, the numbers of persons regarded as lunatic and their location were returned in the annual population censuses and revealed an increase in those in asylums at the expense of those at home and in workhouses: 'there has always been a large mass of insane persons and idiots outside the range of registered lunacy, and that there has been, and still is, greater accuracy in registration, the necessary effect of which is to lessen the reserve lunacy and to increase the registered lunacy, and, therefore to cause an apparent but not real increase of insanity'. Interestingly, the issue of the increase in insanity and the need to make asylum provision for it seems to have occurred later in England and Wales than in Ireland, with the result that many asylums were built in that jurisdiction after 1870 at a time when such activity in Ireland had been largely completed. The shift from workhouse to asylum was similarly later too, so that while, in 1881 in Ireland 77% of lunatics were in asylums and only 13% in workhouses, the respective percentages in England and Wales in 1885 were 67 and 24.

As further influences on increasing institutionalisation of the insane, Tuke, again like his Irish peers, invoked such 'nosocomial' effects as growing acceptability of the asylum among the general public and greater and earlier recognition of mental disease by the medical profession. Another element recognised by Maudsley (1877) was a capitation grant to asylums in respect of each lunatic. 'The Conservative Government had practically offered a premium to parochial authorities for every patient they could, by hook or crook, send into asylums.' Interestingly, in the light of Drapes' comments, Tuke makes passing reference to the increase 'in the proportion of general paralytics' as a factor in the increase. There were very little differences between the two countries in the first admission rate 'exclusive of transfers and re-admissions', being slighter higher for Ireland around 1890 at 6 per 10,000 compared to 5 for England, and the proportion of deaths and discharges as a percentage of the resident population was almost identical at 19%. The earlier and more complete transfer of lunatics from workhouse to asylum went some way towards explaining the greater number of ascertained lunatics in Ireland and did take account of those at large, while such figures were not available for England and Wales.

Finally, it is worth quoting some reflections of Tuke's, not without resonance today, in relation to accumulation or chronicity whether in the hospital or outside of it. 'These results are... nothing to boast of. I say nothing to boast of, because twenty years of social progress and advance of medical knowledge ought to have materially lessened the proportion of insane to the population.' It is also worth noting that another expert, this time from the other side of the Atlantic, Dr Sanborn, writing in the same issue of the Journal, and working with statistics from the Massachusetts State Hospital, came to somewhat different conclusions: 'these facts and inferences are submitted to the judgement of those experts who do not find that 'occurring insanity' is fast gaining as I am sure it is here. If any other interpretation can be put on the figures given, nobody will be more pleased than the writer; but that seems to be hardly possible.'

Back in Ireland, however, we have some idea of the characteristics of those resident in the asylums and, in this respect, nineteenth century Inspectors' reports were more illuminating than those of the first half of the twentieth century. For instance, from that of 1866 we learn that of the 5,070 persons resident at the end of the year, 2,771 suffered from mania, 646 from melancholia, 595 from dementia and 298 from monomania. The remainder were either idiots or imbeciles. The majority, 3,433, were single and, as to their clinical condition, 364 were convalescent, 2,334 were quiet and orderly but insane, 1,352 were moderately tranquil and 1,030 were noisy and refractory. Three hundred and two, only, were well educated, 872 could read and write well, 1,000 could do so only indifferently, 1,491 could not read and 456 were unascertained. As to recovery, 1,254 (40%) were deemed to be probably curable, but the majority, 3,816, were regarded as probably incurable. Of the 22,257 residents in the asylums of England and Wales in 1867, 2,491 (11%) were deemed 'probably curable' (Walton 1983) – Irish asylum doctors were either better therapists or greater optimists. Of those in Irish asylums who were known to be related to each other, 76 were first-degree relatives, i.e. parents, children or siblings, and a further 83 were more distantly related. That the asylum was no idle place was evident from the fact that the majority (59%) of residents were employed on a daily basis. For males the major occupations were garden and farm labour and miscellaneous employment and for women, laundry work, general cleaning and knitting. These nineteenth century reports also contained a wealth of administrative information on such items as the amount of foodstuffs consumed such as oatmeal, mutton, ox heads etc., the number of dormitories, numbers of beds in dormitories, the amount of asylum land in farms cultivated by spade, by plough and a wealth of information on personnel employed, from the resident physician's servant to shoemakers and tailors.

By 1900 the job was done – all known lunatics were in district asylums, none were now at large and only a small number in workhouses. One half of one per cent of the Irish population was to be found in these asylums and the nineteenth century policy of housing the lunatic poor had been accomplished and vindicated. While it is not our purpose to speculate as to the moral and ethical considerations which underpinned confinement, nor to adjudicate between the twin polarities of social convenience and humanitarian impulse, it is perhaps germane to suggest that the nineteenth century's administrators and physicians, in Ireland as elsewhere, satisfied both requirements without necessarily consciously setting out to do so (Scull, 1979). Whatever about these considerations, it was clear that the asylum system had created, in a depressed rural economy, a source of employment for many individuals and families (attendant, medical, maintenance staff and others) who otherwise would have been constrained to emigrate. The establishment of such a reliable economic entity in a local community, despite the popular stigmatising view of the mad and of those who looked after them, and, later, the apprehension that the asylum might contract and disappear, were to lead to resistance to the inauguration of alternative approaches to dealing with the problem of mental illness, as we shall see.

CHAPTER 2

CHAPTER 2

The Consolidation of
Confinement – 1900-1960

In the preceding chapter we have charted the rise of institutionalisation and have followed admission rates as they grew during the 19th century. Now it is time to move to review the 20th century admission scene, first to the apogee in 1958.

During the first decennium of the century the growth in asylum residents continued its 19th century trend and by 1914 there were 16,941 persons resident in the public asylums of the 26 counties. During the years of the First World War numbers resident fell and at year's end in 1918 were down to 15,714, despite the opening in 1916 in the Richmond asylum of a ward for soldiers invalided from the various theatres of war with mental complaints, called the Richmond War Hospital. Soldiers were admitted there without legal formality and the hospital closed at the end of 1919 having treated 362 patients with very satisfactory results; over half of them, reputedly, recovered. By 1919 the number of residents, nationally, had declined further to 15,515, but the inexorable rise once more took over and by 1928, at 17,087, had exceeded the 1914 figure. Thereafter, the increase continued and by 1940 numbers had reached 19,134 before the 'war effect' exerted itself once more, so that at the end of 1945 there were 17,708 resident. Thereafter, once again numbers rose and by 1960 stood at 20,506 (Table 2.1a).

Why, precisely, numbers fell during both world wars is unclear, but it has been a commonplace that in combatant nations in wartime, psychiatric morbidity, and particularly suicide rates, falls. Whatever about the Great War, Ireland was not directly involved in the later conflict, even though some of the consequences, such as food rationing were evident here. Such discomforts, one might have thought, would have increased rather than ameliorated mental state.

In 1923 there were 943 patients resident in private hospitals, roughly one sixteenth of those in district and auxiliary mental hospitals (16,106); by 1960 this figure had become 1,064 (Table 2.2a).

Compared to the earlier century, the 20th century growth in admission numbers was relatively slow, and indeed there was a slight decrease in the first decennium. However, by 1914 numbers of admissions to the district and auxiliary asylums had reached 2,680, of which 537 were recorded as being re-admissions. Similarly to the number of residents, these figures dropped during the First World War to reach 2,393 in 1918. Post-war, the increase began immediately, to 2,743 in 1919, then falling somewhat following this rebound and stabilising with admissions rising by 1930 when admissions stood at 2,348. The next few years showed a relatively static situation until the wartime decline began again, which by 1943 had reached 2,036, with first admissions still predominating at 77% of the total. There was then an enormous spurt in increase in admissions, which by 1948 had reached almost double the figure of four years earlier, with 3,804 being admitted. The comment of the Inspector of Mental Hospitals of the day, somewhat speculatively, was that the increase 'should not be regarded as an increase in the incidence of mental illness in the country. It is an encouraging indication of the growing awareness on the part of the public of the importance of early treatment.' However, it is of importance to note that the Mental Treatment Act of 1945 came into operation on 1 January 1947. This Act allowed for the admission of patients to public hospitals as voluntary patients and in 1948 13.3% of admissions were of this category. Before this legislation there had been provision for admission only to private hospitals of voluntary boarders.

The rush to admission was now well under way and by 1960 there had been a three-fold increase on the 1948 figure reaching 12,555. By now, too, there had been another change: first admissions which in the earlier period had constituted one fifth of all admissions had now swollen to one half; in other words, re-admissions were becoming the order of the day, something that would continue until in the 1990s they constituted three quarters of admissions. As for admissions, so for residents, males exceeded females in a ratio of 5 to 4. Even as late as 1958 and despite the provision for being admitted as voluntary patients the great majority of admissions to district mental hospitals – three quarters – were being admitted under the outdated legislative categorisation of 'of unsound mind'. By contrast, 80% of private admissions were voluntary and 20% of unsound mind.

Given that, particularly in the earlier years, admissions far exceeded discharges – in 1914 2,680 admission to 1,372 discharges and in 1940, 2,241 admissions and 1,125 discharges – it may be asked why did not mental hospital populations grow even more? The answer is of course that the large numbers of deaths created the necessary vacancies for new admissions – 1,116 in 1914 and 1,125 in 1923. So what caused these deaths? The answer in 1914 was a variety of causes but four, pulmonary phthisis (presumably tuberculosis), heart disease, exhaustion from mania or melancholia and atrophy, debility and senile decay, made up more than half of all mortality. By 1940 heart disease and respiratory tuberculosis accounted for 60% of deaths, with old age being accredited with another 12%. In 1960 deaths had fallen to 10% of admissions and to one eighth of discharges.

In 1923 there were 312 admissions to private hospitals, compared to 2,638 to public sector institutions, whereas in 1960 the comparison numbers were 3,410 and 12,555 respectively; therefore in this time period the private sector, in admission terms, grew at twice the rate of the public. In 1923, of 229 discharges from private hospitals, 104 were discharged as recovered; in public hospitals, of 1,362 discharges, 1,005 were deemed recovered. In 1943, of 1,262 discharges from public hospitals, 982 were recovered, and of the 146 discharges from private hospitals, 63 were seen as recovered. Comparable figures are not available for 1960. Obviously the public sector delivered, or believed itself to be delivering, better treatment, or the private sector was more honest. In 1923 the public sector had 1.326 discharges and 1,037 deaths, while the private hospitals had 229 discharges and 61 deaths.

A number of events occurred in the first half of the century of possible significance to mental health care. First by means of the Ministers and Secretaries Act, 1924, asylums were transferred to the control of the Minister for Local Government, with this department being renamed the Department of Local Government and Public Health, second, by means of the Local Government Act of 1925 asylums became mental hospitals. Next, and in the same year, the Minister for Local Government set up a Commission on the Relief of the Sick and Destitute Poor, including the Insane Poor, which reported in 1927. The commissioners were not impressed by the existing provision for the mentally ill in mental hospitals and, among other critical observations, stressed an unacceptable degree of overcrowding which, they felt, could be relieved by the construction of auxiliary hospitals on the lines of that at Youghal, which had been put in place to relieve overcrowding at the Cork (Eglington) asylum. They also recommended that acute mental illness should be treated in general hospitals. They were struck that the legislation covering the field was a hodgepodge of statutes going back to the early 19th century and beyond and recommended a single unifying, consolidating Act including provision for voluntary admission. They also favoured boarding-out as another mechanism to obviate overcrowding and recommended that no hospital should exceed a capacity of 1,000 patients, whereas, at the time, Grangegorman, Portrane, Cork, Ballinasloe and Mullingar exceeded that limit and numbers in the first three were later to rise to 2,000 each. In the event, the only auxiliary hospital to result was at Castlerea where a new branch mental hospital to Ballinasloe was built to accommodate 432 patients in the early 1940s. Its subsequent fate was chequered as it was requisitioned in the 50s as a sanatorium for the treatment of the then rampant tuberculosis, and its residents dispersed to neighbouring hospitals such as Ballinasloe and Castlebar. Some were subsequently recalled when the hospital reverted to psychiatric usage in 1955 and by 1960 it housed 493 patients – 60 more than it was built to contain. Some few of the refugees did not return but remained in the hospitals to which they had been dispersed – some even to this day. From 1955 Castlerea appeared to serve a sanatorium function to neighbouring mental hospitals and tuberculosis patients were transferred there for care of their illness. Even before this the disease was making its impact on mental hospital populations – 303 were recorded as dying from this cause in 1943, and later, in addition to the Castlerea provision, special tuberculosis wards were established in the larger hospitals, as psychiatric patients were not permitted to avail of the general sanatorium provision.

It was to be 1967 before the first general hospital psychiatric unit opened, in Waterford. The legislative response was more immediate with the introduction of the 1945 Mental Treatment Act, which became operative in 1947 and, inter alia, allowed for voluntary admission to hospital and for boarding out, a provision in the event little availed of.

Nothing much else happened during the first half of the 20th century other than that the proportion of the population in asylums or mental hospitals, as they had now become, relative to that outside, increased, partly as a result of continued emigration of those outside hospital (those inside hospital often did not after all have the option of leaving hospital or country). By 1958 the pinnacle had been reached, with approximately 21,000 residents for the 26 counties, representing 0.7% of the population. However there were considerable regional variations, hospital rates generally increasing in progression from east to west and with the highest rate of 1.3% in the Sligo hospital serving the counties of Sligo and Leitrim, reflecting the very high out-migration from the area and the lower likelihood of those already ill and hospitalised to emigrate. These regional variations and their association with various socio-economic indicators had earlier been the subject of study by Dawson (1911), an Inspector at the time. From 1958, resident numbers began to fall year on year and still continue to do so.

Unlike many European counterparts, Ireland was very slow in making separate and specialised provision for those suffering from intellectual disability, or mental defectives as they were called in the earlier days. Indeed, only one such hospital had been provided, Stewart's Institution, by 1900. Under the old administration, concern about the inadequate provision for this group of persons in the United Kingdom was given legislative effect by the introduction of the Mental Deficiency Act, 1913; however, its jurisdiction did not extend to Ireland. In the first half of the 20th century conditions improved with the provision of residential and other services for the intellectually disabled by voluntary bodies– religious orders for the most part. Nevertheless, the burden on psychiatric hospitals continued and, although diagnostic or classificatory information, unlike the position in the former century, is almost completely missing from the early Inspectors' reports, it was clear that mentally handicapped persons were still coming in copious numbers to the psychiatric hospital, either directly from the community or as discards from the voluntary establishments. The first adequate classificatory count of the 20th century did not appear until 1958 and that showed that 11% of hospital residents, or 2,241 persons, were there primarily because they were intellectually disabled, and half (10,670) were classified as schizophrenic. Anecdotal reports by many hospital superintendents confirmed that many such were still being referred from a variety of sources for admission, often at very young ages.

A further point of difficulty for those attempting to provide services of some quality was the lack of control they had over referral sources; they evidently believed that they had to admit whoever was referred to them and were aware that if they refused admission to any referral however unsuitable, and some disaster ensued, they would receive scant mercy in official quarters. A particular difficulty for them was having to accept, on transfer from former poor law and other institutions, elderly persons with senile decline, who they felt did not require mental hospital care. In 1960 one-fifth of all admission were over age 65. Frequently, admissions came from homes for unmarried mothers or similar locations of persons who did not conform to the mores of these institutions.

Another problem was that few of the attendant or nursing staff had any formal training and it was to be the 1950s before this situation improved. The extent of effective therapies was, in the first half of the century, limited and this no doubt did little to lift despondency. It is true that malarial therapy had been introduced for neurosyphilis and that the numbers of persons dying from the associated general paralysis of the insane in psychiatric hospitals had begun to decline – there had been 11 such deaths in 1943 – but one had to wait for the introduction of penicillin a decade or more later to see syphilis no longer a cause of psychiatric hospitalisation. Electroconvulsive therapy, insulin coma therapy – the one now less frequently used and the other abandoned – antipsychotics and antidepressants were to be treatments of the next generation.

Overall, the mood of service providers in the early 20th century was gloomy. Attempts to improve conditions in hospitals were frequently frustrated by lack of funding and what many saw as obstructionism as a means to keep costs down. That such constraints were not entirely the devices of local management may be gleaned from the following comment of two members of the committee of Grangegorman in 1932, as quoted by Reynolds (1992): 'there is perhaps no more sorrowful journey in the world today than the three or four hours necessary to inspect an institution like Grangegorman'. A quarter of a century later the medical superintendent of the same hospital was moved to state 'I am compelled to say at this stage that the overcrowded conditions for our patients in St Brendan's (as Grangegorman had now become) are contrary to every modern idea of human society.' Central government was always seen as scrimping and scraping for fear that any increased burden on rates might ensue and saw it as its duty to oppose automatically any proposed initiative. That the psychiatric services were not greatly favoured in funding was apparent from the fact that, of the £35 million disbursed from the Sweepstakes Fund to hospitals less than £1.5 million came to the psychiatric hospitals. Notwithstanding, the high cost of hospitalisation was reflected by the fact that in the financial year of 1960/61, of the total non-capital health service expenditure of £19,479,490, the psychiatric component was £4,050,800 or 20.8%. By 1975 psychiatric expenditure had risen to £28,697,000 of £103,241,700, but in proportional terms had fallen to 14.85%. From 1954 to 1977 the expenditure on mental health per head of population rose from £6.9 to £68.4.

Perhaps the most significant comment on which to close this review of the growth of institutionalisation in the 20th century is the comment of the Inspector of Mental Hospitals, in 1960, tongue in cheek, no doubt, 'The uphill struggle to modernise these hospitals, to relieve overcrowding and to achieve a satisfactory standard continues, but there is still a long way to go before our services can be regarded as adequate.'

CHAPTER 3

CHAPTER 3

In-patient Activity, Admissions
and Discharges – 1960-2002

In 1961 a Commission on Mental Illness was set up to review the mental health services in Ireland and make recommendations for their improvement. The Commission, intrigued by the extraordinarily high rate of psychiatric hospitalisation in the country, attempted to research whether this reflected raised mental illness rates in the Irish and found that it could not do so because of data limitations (Department of Health, 1966). Instead, the Commission recommended that the matter should be explored by the Medico Social Research Board (MSRB), shortly to be set up.

At the behest of the Commission of Inquiry on Mental Illness the Department had instigated an inpatient reporting system in psychiatric hospitals. It had begun with a census of all residents on the 31 March 1963 whose details were recorded on a sheet individual to each resident. No personal details were entered on the sheet, instead a hospital number was allocated to each and this was to be regarded as a personal identifier. The sheet was to be completed on every admission subsequent to midnight 31 March, and in the case of persons discharged and re-admitted and therefore already in the system, they were to be identified by their hospital number. Because the system was national rather than local, newly admitted patients or their relatives were asked if they had ever been psychiatrically hospitalised elsewhere, and if they had, a phone call would be made to the relevant hospital to ascertain their hospital number in that hospital and the records collated. The accumulated sheets from census day onwards were sent from the Department to the MSRB in 1969 and were worked on by the mental health unit. The outcome was the 1963 Psychiatric Hospital Census published in 1971 (Walsh, 1971). An analysis of the sheets for admissions, discharges and deaths resulted in the composite publication *Activities of Irish Psychiatric Hospitals and Units 1965–1969* (O'Hare & Walsh, 1972). This was followed by a report for the single year 1970 (O'Hare & Walsh, 1974a).

On the 31 March 1971, as part of the newly introduced National Psychiatric In-patient Reporting System (NPIRS), a new reporting form devised by the MSRB mental health unit was introduced with a midnight census. Among other improvements, the new form requested that diagnoses be returned in accordance with the eighth revision of the International Classification of Diseases (ICD) (WHO, 1974). The previous diagnostic classificatory system devised by the Commission did not correspond to any recognised nosology, being merely a very broad grouping of major categories. Nevertheless, these categories were convertible to the ICD eighth revision to allow the first three months of 1971 to be amalgamated with the last nine, to allow presentation of the 1971 Activities report as a unit together with that of 1972 in a joint publication for the two years. Thereafter, the Activities reports have appeared on an annual basis, with updating of the diagnostic categories as the ICD has evolved and is now in its tenth edition (WHO, 1992). Likewise, as the Irish Classification of Occupations has changed, this has been taken into account. Finally, from the outset at the 1971 census, an attempt was made to record-link the system using a set of personal identifiers, such as date and place of birth, to allow follow-up of cohorts of patients and for example to, distinguish between re-admissions and individuals contributing to these re-admissions. Subsequently, on ethical grounds of confidentiality, the record-linkage operation was abandoned.

NPIRS produced more information about inpatient activity than had been available hitherto and from 1971 onwards it became possible to produce detailed information on a range of parameters. This is now presented for all admissions, first admissions and discharges. The main and more interesting data are interspersed with text commentary, while the more detailed tabular data are relegated to the appendix.

All admissions
(first and re-admissions combined)

All admission numbers increased over the 37-year period, from 15,440 in 1965 to 23,736 in 2002. However, within this time span there were considerable fluctuations. Admission numbers reached a peak in 1986 at 29,392 and have been steadily declining ever since. Rates of admission over the 37-year period also fluctuated greatly (Figure 3.1 and Table 3.1a). Rates increased steadily in the early years, from 535.4 per 100,000 in 1965 to a rate of 928.8 per 100,000 in 1978. The rates varied somewhat in the following years and from 1991 onwards rates have been steadily decreasing with the exception of 1996. Over the entire 37-year period, rates increased from 535.4 in 1965 to 605.9 per 100,000 in 2002.

Gender

The male admission rate was higher than the female admission rate over the entire 37-year period (Table 3.1). (For all years see Table 3.2a). Over the course of the 37-year period, the male rate increased from 551.2 in 1965, its lowest point, to 629.2.2 per 100,000 population in 2002. The male rate reached a peak in 1978 with a rate of 1,010.1 per 100,000 population. Similarly, the female rate increased over the 37-year period from 519.4 in 1965, again the lowest rate, to 583.0 per 100,000 population in 2002. It, too, peaked in 1978, with a rate of 846.6 per 100,000 population.

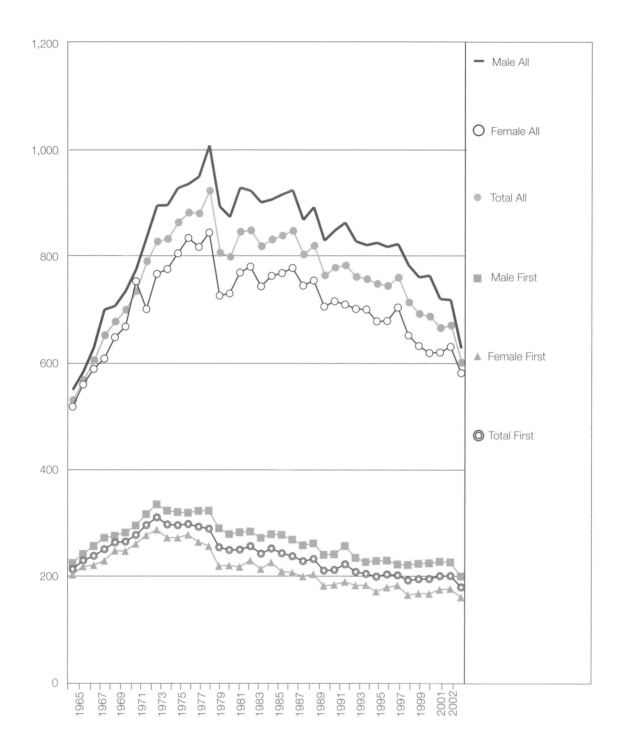

Figure 3.1 All and first admission rates 1965-2002

Table 3.1 All and first admissions by gender for various years 1965–2002. Rates per 100,000 total population.

	All			First		
	Male	Female	Total	Male	Female	Total
1965	551.2	519.4	535.4	226.2	204.3	215.3
1970	736.6	670.0	705.3	283.4	248.5	266.9
1975	930.4	807.7	869.3	321.9	273.6	297.9
1980	875.9	732.2	804.5	280.3	221.6	251.1
1985	918.0	770.4	844.5	279.2	210.7	245.1
1990	850.7	717.7	784.2	242.6	185.4	214.0
1995	819.8	680.8	749.9	230.8	180.5	205.5
2000	721.9	621.5	671.3	228.7	176.4	202.4
2002	629.2	583.0	605.9	201.3	162.0	181.5

Age

The 35–44 year age group had the highest admission rate for all years up to 1988 with only two exceptions, in 1967 and 1979 (Table 3.2). (For all years see Table 3.3a). From 1989 to 2002, the 45–54 year age group had the highest rate of admission.

Table 3.2 All admissions by age for various years 1965–2002. Rates per 100,000 total population.

	< 15	15–19	20–24	25–34	35–44	45–54	55–64	65–69	70–79
1965	19.0	209.4	513.3	913.7	952.7	905.4	940.9	902.6	786.1
1970	15.4	304.2	810.6	1,173.9	1,250.5	1,185.6	1,221.5	1,132.0	964.0
								65–74	75&over
1975	15.8	300.3	882.6	1,592.0	1,763.5	1,517.8	1,425.6	1,236.5	825.4
1980	14.5	210.7	648.5	1,146.3	1,659.9	1,618.0	1,451.2	1,376.6	1,024.7
1985	10.7	204.6	646.8	1,188.4	1,768.9	1,657.8	1,588.5	1,444.3	1,106.1
1990	11.1	228.9	576.1	1,111.9	1,481.9	1,563.8	1,379.2	1,235.4	1,101.8
1995	35.0	184.0	565.7	815.3	1,100.5	1,282.6	1,164.0	1,178.3	996.6
2000	9.7[a]	302.5	713.5	933.7	1,099.1	1,129.2	1,067.3	851.9	681.3
2002	8.1[a]	294.5	587.8	758.1	932.9	982.6	908.3	800.1	607.7

a under 16s.

Marital status

Rates for marital status were extracted for 1971 to 2002 (Table 3.3). (For all years see Table 3.4a). Admission rates were highest for widowed persons for all years up to 1999, with rates in excess of 1,000 per 100,000 population from 1971 to 1995. In 2000 and 2001 divorced persons had the highest rate of admission.

Table 3.3 All admissions by marital status for various years 1965–2002. Numbers and rates per 100,000 total population.

	Numbers					Rates				
	S	M	W	D	U	S	M	W	D	U
1965	8,553	5,486	1,395	-	6	-	-	-	-	-
1970	10,504	7,907	1,798	-	133	-	-	-	-	-
1975	12,633	10,965	2,059	-	235	713.1	1,056.3	1,218.9	-	-
1980	12,837	11,377	2,214	-	670	660.6	912.6	1,240.4	-	-
1985	14,235	11,229	2,372	-	1,246	720.5	871.8	1,320.5	-	-
1990	14,022	9,689	2,113	-	1,941	696.6	743.0	1,134.1	-	-
1995	14,162	7,948	1,905	-	2,425	725.0	597.9	1,014.9	-	-
2000	13,269	6,990	1,393	86	2,605	664.4	515.3	755.4	878.7	-
2002	12,809	6,805	1,224	220	2,678	598.0	467.9	655.0	627.5	-

S=Single M=Married W=Widowed D=Divorced U=Unspecified.

Socio-economic group

Data on socio-economic groups for the years 1971 to 2002 are presented in Table 3.5a in the Appendix, with data for various years presented in Table 3.4. Accurate and reliable socio-economic data were not available for the years 1965–1970. Admission rates from 1971 to 2002 show the 'unskilled' group having the highest rate of admission, with one exception in 1971. Rates for the unskilled increased substantially during the 1980s with rates in excess of 2,000 per 100,000 population, reaching a peak in 1986 with a rate of 2,368.6 per 100,000. In 1989, the rate of admission for the unskilled group was eleven times that of the lowest rated group, employers and managers. The employers and managers group has had the lowest rate of admission of all socio-economic groups from 1976 to 1999, reaching a low of 114.4 per 100,000 population in 1997. This contrasts with rates in excess of 500 per 100,000 in the early years. In 2000, 2001 and 2002 own-account workers (self-employed persons with employees) have had the lowest rate of admission, at 42.3, 118.6 and 111.2 per 100,000 population respectively. Skilled workers have had the second lowest rates of admission from 1990 to 1999 (with one exception in 1997), with rates ranging from 453.7 in 1990 to 308.4 per 100,000 population in 1999. Rates of admission for most of the socio-economic groups have decreased from the first year of recording in 1971 to the present date.

Table 3.4   All admissions by socio-economic group for various years 1965–2002. Rates per 100,000 total population.

	F	OA	HP	LP	EM	SE	INM	ONM	SM	SS	US
1971	460.2	915.2	836.6	908.4	477.1	427.6	546.5	880.5	422.5	628.4	832.7
1975	722.7	1,153.6	1,024.9	987.3	581.6	518.9	941.1	1,292.9	728.6	631.2	1,796.5
1980	641.3	975.1	796.4	930.5	345.1	709.7	950.3	1,057.7	652.8	853.4	1,621.6
1985	901.9	1,113.3	612.2	749.4	440.8	538.6	922.0	1,093.0	543.5	989.2	2,360.9
1990	706.1	725.8	490.2	576.3	237.5	458.4	672.4	843.7	453.7	906.0	2,103.0
1995	531.7	546.6	534.7	462.6	197.5	564.2	413.5	683.0	393.7	962.8	1,112.5
	F	AW	HP	LP	EM	OAW	NM		MS	SS	US
2000	399.9	313.3	322.8	501.1	168.2	42.3	442.2		388.2	288.1	883.2
2002	391.6	553.9	363.8	408.7	115.9	111.2	479.6		650.1	478.4	1,236.6

F=Farmers OA=Other Agricultural Workers HP=Higher Professional LP=Lower Professional EM=Employers & Managers SE=Salaried Employees INM=Intermediate Non-Manual ONM=Other Non-Manual SM=Skilled Manual SS=Semi-Skilled US=Unskilled AW=Agricultural Workers OAW=Own-account Workers NM=Non-manual MS=Manual Skilled.

Diagnosis

Examination of admission rates by diagnosis over the 37-year period points to the emergence of three main diagnoses on admission, namely schizophrenia, affective disorders and alcoholic disorders. All three have had consistently higher rates of admission compared to all other diagnostic groups and have accounted for two-thirds of all admissions. Despite increases in the rate of admission for schizophrenia in the early years up to 1976, rates have been decreasing since then, with an overall 47% reduction in rates from 1971 (227.9) to 2002 (120.5) (Table 3.6a). Rates of admission for affective disorders have increased by over one-third – from 203.3 in 1971 to 275.9 in 2002. Rates of admission for alcoholic disorders increased considerably over the 37-year period, from 56.8 in 1965 to 101.0 per 100,000 population in 2002, reaching a peak in 1978 with a rate of 244.8 per 100,000 population.

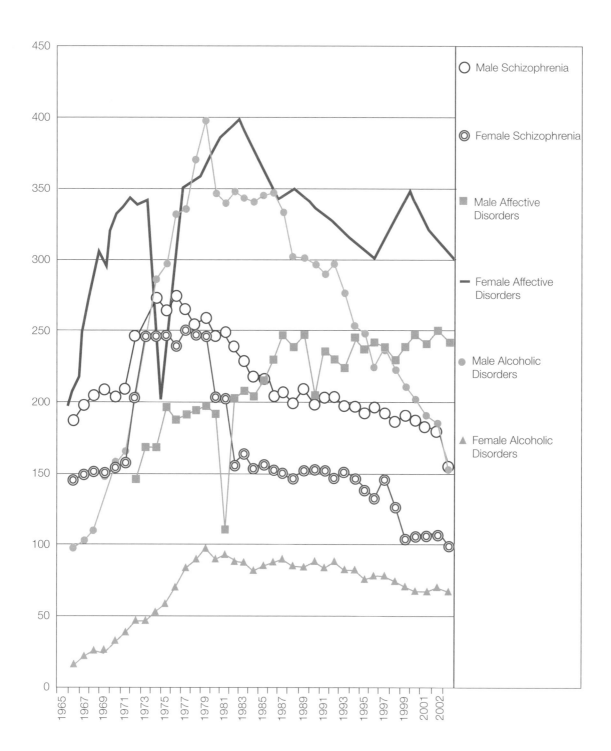

Figure 3.2 All admission rates, by gender, for schizophrenia, affective disorders and alcoholic disorders. Ireland 1965-2002

Figure 3.2 presents all admissions rates by gender for schizophrenia, alcoholic disorders and affective disorders (see also Table 3.7a). The male rate for alcoholic disorders was considerably higher than that for the other disorders from 1972 to the late 1980s, with admission rates reaching a peak in 1978, at 398.9 per 100,000 population. Despite this, the male to female admission ratio for alcoholic disorders decreased from 6:1 in 1968 to 2:1 in 2002. Although the male rate for alcoholic disorders has been consistently higher than the female rate over the 37-year period, there has been a gradual decline in the rate over this period. Rates of admission for female affective disorders have been consistently higher than those for males. However, in recent years the male rate has been increasing, from 221.6 in 1997 to 236.3 in 2002. Admission patterns for schizophrenia show males having a consistently higher rate of admission than females for the entire 37-year period.

Legal status

The rate of non-voluntary all admission decreased from 130.0 in 1971 to 69.4 in 2002 (Table 3.5). (See also Table 3.8a), while the proportion of non-voluntary admissions decreased by 6% for the same period. Males had a consistently higher rate and proportion of non-voluntary admission compared to females from 1971 to 2002.

Table 3.5   Non-voluntary all admissions 1971-2002. Percentages and rates per 100,000 total population.

	Male	Female	Total	Male	Female	Total
	%			Rates		
1971	18.9	16.0	17.6	147.1	112.8	130.0
1973	18.6	14.0	16.5	166.6	108.0	137.4
1975	17.0	14.2	15.7	157.7	114.4	136.2
1977	16.7	12.9	15.0	159.1	105.8	132.6
1979	15.2	11.7	13.6	153.7	96.5	125.2
1981	13.6	10.5	12.2	143.5	91.1	117.4
1983	13.8	10.9	12.5	124.8	81.2	103.1
1985	13.4	11.1	12.3	122.8	85.2	104.1
1987	12.6	9.7	11.3	108.7	72.1	90.5
1989	13.9	12.0	13.0	115.8	85.0	100.4
1991	13.0	10.2	11.7	112.3	72.9	92.6
1993	12.5	9.3	11.0	102.9	65.2	84.0
1995	12.1	9.4	10.9	98.9	64.2	81.5
1997	12.3	9.3	10.9	96.5	61.0	78.6
1999	12.2	9.3	10.9	93.2	57.8	75.3
2002	12.8	10.0	11.4	80.5	58.3	69.4

Health board areas

Admission rates were highest for the Mid-Western Health Board for much of the late 1970s to the late 1980s (Table 3.6 and Table 3.9a). Thereafter until the early 1990s rates were highest in the South-Eastern Health Board, with the North-Western Health Board having the highest rates in the mid to late 1990s. In 2000 and 2001 admissions rates were highest in the Midland Health Board, while in 2002 rates were highest in the South-Eastern Health Board once again. The North-Eastern Health Board had the lowest rate of admission from 1981 to 2002. Admission rates over the 37-year period increased in the Midland Health Board, from 708.7 in 1972 to 725.9 in 2002, and there was a marginal increase in the Western Health Board, from 703.4 in 1972 to 704.4 in 2002.

Table 3.6   All admission rates by health board area 1972–2002. Rates per 100,000 total population.

	EHB/ERHA	MHB	MWHB	NEHB	NWHB	SEHB	SHB	WHB
1972	827.8	708.7	846.6	684.2	773.1	912.5	752.7	703.4
1973	862.1	651.5	884.8	705.8	775.8	925.6	816.5	793.7
1975	865.6	667.9	1,042.2	763.6	917.7	1,015.2	793.9	807.3
1977	865.3	766.8	1,079.3	824.7	996.9	1,026.7	818.6	738.4
1979	759.1	749.1	954.1	777.3	1,050.9	993.2	626.7	834.1
1981	735.2	803.7	1,128.9	709.3	1,076.8	991.8	788.0	922.7
1983	718.3	838.0	1,102.4	648.4	915.4	977.9	774.7	918.7
1985	761.5	816.2	1,120.9	655.0	869.8	1,010.2	795.4	906.1
1987	803.3	726.7	997.3	624.6	931.9	949.8	676.8	864.8
1989	774.5	823.6	860.7	610.2	758.7	892.8	642.0	818.8
1991	801.4	695.2	766.2	637.3	825.4	906.0	723.4	856.7
1993	794.7	654.8	722.2	532.1	903.4	797.7	711.3	881.1
1995	789.8	698.1	720.6	514.4	880.5	783.7	695.3	799.8
1997	744.2	732.2	671.1	473.0	855.5	754.8	668.8	799.5
1999	726.2	784.8	631.7	435.4	757.3	786.4	587.8	781.6
2002	588.8	725.9	558.0	352.8	649.9	730.6	591.5	704.4

Legal status by health board areas

The Western Health Board had, without exception, the highest rate of non-voluntary admission from 1989–1999 (Table 3.7), while the Southern Health Board had the highest rate from 2000 to 2002. It is noteworthy that, in the period from 1989 to 2002, the rate in the Southern Health Board increased by 23% while that of the Midland Health Board decreased by 61% and the Western Health Board has decreased by 39%. The North-Eastern Health Board, on the other hand, had the lowest rate of non-voluntary admission for all but one year between 1989 and 2002.

Table 3.7   Non-voluntary admissions (all) by health board area 1989–2002. Rates per 100,000 total population.

	EHB/ERHA	MHB	MWHB	NEHB	NWHB	SEHB	SHB	WHB
1989	99.7	142.8	90.0	71.8	102.9	89.1	76.6	153.0
1990	80.2	118.3	94.5	62.9	102.5	81.3	77.3	141.5
1991	86.3	106.3	88.8	63.6	103.4	69.1	92.4	142.1
1992	77.1	104.8	83.7	64.9	84.1	56.9	82.0	129.8
1993	73.2	109.1	70.1	63.2	87.9	67.8	89.0	136.9
1994	73.8	89.9	86.5	53.3	100.6	68.1	87.2	121.7
1995	73.6	72.4	81.1	49.3	86.0	72.8	88.1	127.7
1996	68.1	84.7	102.7	54.6	104.7	77.8	85.3	144.9
1997	65.4	87.1	94.0	48.7	75.9	53.2	113.7	130.8
1998	56.4	68.6	81.4	48.7	73.5	51.8	108.3	111.5
1999	67.2	74.0	81.7	41.8	93.4	59.8	96.3	110.1
2000	60.0	68.1	81.1	45.1	90.6	51.0	133.1	83.2
2001	65.6	77.8	84.2	42.5	98.2	43.0	123.1	90.0
2002	56.7	55.9	88.9	38.3	79.4	61.8	94.6	93.1

Hospital type

Table 3.8 (see Table 3.10a for all years) shows the percentage of admissions by hospital type from 1965 to 2002. The proportion of admissions to health board psychiatric hospitals decreased over the last 37 years, from 75% to 41%, while that for general hospital psychiatric units increased from 0% in 1965 to 41% of all admissions in 2002. This increase in admissions to general hospital units is a reflection of the opening of such facilities in tandem with the closure of admission units in psychiatric hospitals.

Table 3.8 All admissions by hospital type for various years 1965-2002. Percentages.

	Local authority/health board psychiatric hospitals	General hospital units	Private hospitals	Children's centres
1965	75.9	0.0	24.1	0.0
1970	74.3	4.6	21.1	0.0
1975	71.0	10.9	18.0	0.2
1980	67.2	15.4	17.1	0.3
1985	68.7	16.2	14.7	0.3
1990	62.4	20.5	16.5	0.5
1995	53.9	28.9	16.1	1.2
2000	46.8	39.1	13.9	0.3
2002	41.0	41.1	17.6	0.2

First admissions

The definition of first admissions as issued to hospitals for the purposes of NPIRS was: first ever admission to the receiving hospital or unit, and any prior admission to any inpatient facility, wherever located, for however short a time, disqualified an admission from being returned as a first admission. This was to ensure that persons were not regarded as first admissions who had experienced an earlier admission to another hospital but who were experiencing a first admission to the returning hospital.

It is instructive to compare admission numbers between 1892 and 2002. The total admission numbers for the 32 counties in 1892 were 3,182, with 2,415 first admissions. The 26 county figures for 2002 were 23,736 and 7,111 respectively. The far higher proportion of first admissions earlier is noteworthy, as is the much lower ratio between first and re-admissions between the two years. If one assumes that most of those first admitted in 1892 were suffering from severe, i.e. psychotic illness (and assumes that these comprised what is now called schizophrenia and psychotic depression – a point difficult to verify) and restricts the 2002 first admissions to those psychotically ill, 758 with schizophrenia (psychotic depression, or, to use the 19th century term, involutional melancholia, having largely disappeared), it is possible that there would be little discrepancy between the figures. But for the moment let us confine ourselves to more recent times and less speculative issues.

First admission numbers have increased over the 37-year period, from 6,210 in 1965 to 7,111 in 2002 (Figure 3.1). They reached a peak of 9,018 in 1973 and have fluctuated considerably since then (Table 3.1a). Rates reached a peak of 312.6 per 100,000 in 1973, fluctuating thereafter and decreasing to 181.5 per 100,000 in 2002.

Gender

The male first admission rate was higher than the female rate for the entire 37-year period (Table 3.2a). The male rate increased in the early years, from 226.2 in 1965 to a peak of 336.2 per 100,000 population in 1973. On the whole, rates have been decreasing since then, to 201.3 per 100,000 population in 2002. The female rate decreased from 204.3 per 100,000 population in 1965 to 162.0 per 100,000 population in 2002. It peaked in 1973 with a rate of 288.8 per 100,000 population.

Age

Age at admission varied somewhat over the 37 years with the 25–34-year age group having the highest rates of admission for the most part in the 1960s and the 1970s with three exceptions (Table 3.9 and Table 3.11a for all years). For much of the 1980s and the early 1990s the 35–44-year age group had the highest rate of admission with the 75-and-over age group having the highest rate from 1994 to 1996. From 1997 to 2000 the 25–34-year age group once again had the highest rates of admission, with the 35–44-year age group having the highest rate in 2001 and 2002.

Table 3.9   First admissions by age for various years 1965–2002. Rates per 100,000 total population.

	< 15	15–19	20–24	25–34	35–44	45–54	55–64	65–69	70–79	80 & over
1965	10.4	132.3	252.0	367.0	344.1	320.7	335.9	349.3	366.9	341.8
1970	9.6	189.3	379.9	467.7	424.7	382.8	394.6	396.6	411.4	413.4
								65–74	75&Over	
1975	9.7	180.7	398.6	587.9	532.7	449.5	407.3	400.9	393.0	
1980	9.8	124.4	287.3	389.6	479.0	422.1	334.2	391.2	480.2	
1985	7.9	127.1	285.7	385.7	480.8	377.4	333.3	380.0	438.9	
1990	6.1	129.3	252.4	332.8	370.4	349.9	288.5	275.3	348.3	
1995	10.4	119.1	314.7	315.1	315.2	300.1	242.5	254.5	327.3	
2000	7.9	172.5	299.0	325.0	293.9	272.3	243.0	211.0	244.1	
2002	6.9	171.2	256.4	248.8	258.7	238.9	202.8	202.8	218.0	

Marital status

As with all admissions, widowed persons had the highest rate of first admissions for all years up to 1999, with divorced persons having the highest rate from 2000 to 2002 (Table 3.10 and Table 3.12a for all years).

Table 3.10 First admissions by marital status for various years 1965–2002. Numbers and rates per 100,000 total population.

	Numbers					Rates				
	S	M	W	D	U	S	M	W	D	U
1965	3,310	2,317	583	-	-	-	-	-	-	-
1970	3,683	3,221	739	-	53	-	-	-	-	-
1975	4,119	3,967	705	-	82	232.5	382.1	417.3	-	-
1980	3,744	3,730	731	-	254	192.7	299.2	409.6	-	-
1985	3,803	3,565	694	-	379	192.5	276.8	386.4	-	-
1990	3,601	2,886	551	-	539	178.9	221.3	295.7	-	-
1995	3,753	2,378	486	-	629	192.1	178.9	258.9	-	-
2000	3,959	2,202	400	32	745	198.2	162.3	216.9	327.0	-
2002	3,766	2,182	368	78	717	175.8	150.0	196.9	222.5	-

S=Single M=Married W=Widowed D=Divorced U=Unspecified.

Socio-economic group

As with all admissions, data on socio-economic group were not available for first admissions prior to 1971. Similarly to all admissions, the unskilled group had the highest rate of first admissions compared to all other socio-economic groups in all years with the exception of 1971 and 1972 the first two years (Table 3.11 for various years and Table 3.13a for all years). In 1983 and in 1989 the rate of admission for the unskilled group was six times that of the employers and managers group. However, this differential has been decreasing since. The rate of admission for the unskilled group reached a peak in 1984, with at 585.6 per 100,000 population.

Table 3.11 First admissions by socio-economic group for various years 1971-2002. Rates per 100,000 total population.

	F	OA	HP	LP	EM	SE	INM	ONM	SM	SS	US	UNS
1971	160.6	268.3	387.1	423.3	206.4	192.2	225.4	288.3	173.0	229.5	264.8	1,452.8
1975	229.0	284.8	464.3	408.6	240.7	194.8	345.8	396.3	270.6	214.2	583.0	46.9
1980	170.2	252.5	326.4	342.1	141.1	261.3	327.9	290.3	229.1	238.3	448.7	131.7
1985	218.9	269.8	222.3	243.2	159.1	184.4	292.6	290.9	183.3	276.0	565.4	129.2
1990	153.6	165.2	176.9	193.4	88.7	157.5	213.3	221.4	140.1	218.2	481.9	398.5
1995	118.5	139.2	153.3	140.2	60.5	228.0	117.3	187.8	114.3	270.5	219.0	699.4
	F	AW	HP	LP	EM	OAW	NM		MS	SS	US	UNS
2000	85.4	69.5	113.2	191.5	65.2	16.7	129.6		136.5	89.5	215.1	845.1
2002	103.4	121.2	138.7	141.9	46.8	37.6	150.1		223.5	139.9	264.8	403.4

F=Farmers OA=Other Agricultural Workers HP=Higher Professional LP=Lower Professional EM=Employers & Managers SE=Salaried Employees INM=Intermediate Non-Manual ONM=Other Non-Manual SM=Skilled Manual SS=Semi-Skilled US=Unskilled UNS=Unspecified AW=Agricultural Workers OAW=Own Account Workers NM=Non-manual MS=Manual Skilled.

Diagnosis

The peak first admission rate for schizophrenia was 78.4 per 100,000 population in 1973 and thereafter has fallen continuously to less than half that rate, at 23.2 in 2002 (Table 3.14a). Does this reflect a real decline in the condition or simply the fact that more cases are being treated exclusively in the community and never come to hospital? All prior wisdom has suggested that because of the seriousness of the illness and its social consequences all cases will at some time or other in their lifetime come to in-patient care. If this is so, there should be a shift in the age at first admission towards older age groups from 1973 to 2002, and this is so after age 54.[1] The fall in first admission rates for schizophrenia was greater in males (Table 3.15a) and in the older age groups. The other possibility, that the decline is due to a lesser propensity on the part of clinicians to diagnose schizophrenia, should be reflected in a compensatory increase in other similar conditions, but this has not occurred.

As far as other diagnostic groups are concerned we have limited our scrutiny to alcohol disorders and affective illnesses. First admission rates for alcohol disorders increased from 24.2 per 100,000 population in 1965 to 85.2 in 1978 and have since fallen to 36.1 in 2002 (Table 3.14a). These changes are consonant with; during the earlier period, the remarkable increase in alcohol consumption (Department of Health and Children, 2003a) and, more recently, the move to deal with alcohol problems on a community basis with specialised services. As far as affective disorders are concerned, these rates have increased by almost one quarter, from 68.8 per 100,000 in 1971 to 83.0 in 2002.

---

1 Based on analysis of NPIRS data from 1973 to 2002.

Legal status

There was a reduction in the rate of non-voluntary first admissions by over half from 57.1 in 1971 to 24.5 per 100,000 in 2002 (Table 3.12 and Table 3.16a) Likewise, the rate for males and females also fell by over half for this time period.

Table 3.12   Non-voluntary first admissions by gender for various years 1971-2002. Rates per 100,000 total population.

	Male	Female	Total
1971	62.9	51.2	57.1
1975	63.3	47.8	55.6
1980	44.5	34.0	39.3
1985	46.0	32.7	39.4
1990	35.3	21.5	28.4
1995	36.8	20.0	28.4
2000	32.1	20.5	26.3
2002	29.3	19.6	24.5

Health board areas

The North-Eastern Health Board has had one of the lowest first admission rates since the 1970s and one of the largest percentage reductions in rates over this time, at 49% (Table 3.13 and Table 3.17a). The Mid-Western Health Board had the largest percentage reduction in rates since 1972, at 52%. First admission rates have changed little in the Western Health Board, with a reduction of only 12% between 1972 and 2002.

Legal status by health board area

The Western Health Board had the highest rate of non-voluntary admission for all but four years from 1989 to 2002 (Table 3.14). From 2000 to 2002 the Southern Health Board had the highest rate of non-voluntary admission, with increases in rates on previous years.

Table 3.13 First admissions by health board areas for various years 1972–2002. Rates per 100,000 total population.

	EHB/ERHA	MHB	MWHB	NEHB	NWHB	SEHB	SHB	WHB
1972	327.7	278.3	304.3	240.9	223.2	335.4	295.4	244.5
1973	339.1	236.8	338.3	238.3	222.7	331.0	315.3	304.5
1975	298.0	243.7	378.0	259.4	237.9	335.3	298.5	259.3
1977	300.1	264.3	336.9	253.3	279.1	322.8	295.0	246.5
1979	251.5	260.1	270.2	214.9	247.5	309.1	227.8	258.0
1981	241.1	254.1	305.1	191.4	250.9	280.5	247.4	245.2
1983	231.2	257.2	280.6	191.3	233.9	280.8	237.6	259.5
1985	240.7	239.9	295.5	172.3	203.6	274.4	233.6	268.0
1987	255.4	202.3	254.0	175.0	188.7	236.2	193.2	237.8
1989	230.3	195.2	250.4	160.9	184.3	212.0	186.4	214.5
1991	227.2	181.3	228.3	198.7	213.4	223.9	241.9	219.0
1993	223.6	174.0	172.1	179.4	194.1	196.1	182.7	258.4
1995	217.9	205.9	182.2	169.6	183.0	199.9	195.4	224.2
1997	206.5	196.1	169.4	146.0	193.0	192.6	181.8	215.7
1999	212.5	206.3	163.4	137.8	173.1	216.8	170.7	228.2
2002	175.6	202.3	147.2	122.3	165.6	206.1	198.7	214.8
% reduction in rates	46.4	27.3	51.6	49.2	25.8	38.6	32.7	12.1

Hospital type

Table 3.15 presents the percentage of first admissions by hospital type for various years from 1965 to 2002 (see Table 3.18a for all years). The proportion of first admissions to health board psychiatric hospitals has decreased from 69% in 1965 to 36% in 2001. There was an increase in admissions to general hospital psychiatric units from 0% in 1965 to 41% in 2002. As with all admissions, this increase is a reflection of the opening of more general hospital psychiatric facilities in tandem with the closure of the larger, more traditional psychiatric hospital and the increase in community facilities.

Table 3.14 Non-voluntary first admissions by health board area 1989–2002. Rates per 100,000 total population.

	EHB/ERHA	MHB	MWHB	NEHB	NWHB	SEHB	SHB	WHB
1989	37.6	48.6	28.5	23.2	32.4	28.3	23.1	41.9
1990	26.6	33.7	30.8	21.9	23.5	27.5	24.2	41.3
1991	28.4	32.7	30.8	23.2	32.4	26.0	37.3	46.5
1992	23.7	30.3	24.4	19.9	22.1	17.1	25.1	46.5
1993	22.0	38.0	19.3	24.2	25.9	21.0	28.9	39.3
1994	27.0	30.8	21.2	18.9	20.2	22.6	27.0	43.1
1995	27.7	28.1	25.7	20.0	19.7	25.1	28.7	39.4
1996	26.9	26.1	35.7	21.7	24.0	27.9	28.9	40.8
1997	23.8	29.7	30.0	18.3	19.9	18.3	35.8	43.7
1998	21.5	23.8	28.1	16.3	17.5	17.4	31.7	38.6
1999	27.9	25.8	24.9	15.4	26.6	19.2	35.5	39.7
2000	23.6	21.4	25.5	20.3	23.2	20.5	48.8	26.7
2001	21.7	23.8	20.8	13.1	28.5	17.2	49.0	24.4
2002	21.8	17.3	28.3	15.1	19.4	20.8	35.5	28.9

Table 3.15 First admissions by hospital type for various years 1965–2002. Percentages.

	Local authority/ health board psychiatric hospitals	General hospital units	Private hospitals	Unspecified	Children's centres
1965	69.3	0.0	30.7	0.0	0.0
1970	64.5	8.0	27.5	0.0	0.0
1975	63.9	13.0	22.8	0.0	0.3
1980	59.4	16.7	23.1	0.0	0.8
1985	63.5	17.7	18.0	0.0	0.9
1990	56.2	21.2	21.6	0.0	1.1
1995	48.3	30.0	20.8	0.0	0.8
2000	40.2	40.9	18.3	0.0	0.7
2002	35.5	41.1	22.7	0.0	0.7

County of residence

By examining admissions by county of residence for 2001 it was hoped to establish which counties were contributing to the higher admission rates in individual health boards. There were considerable differences in the rate of all admissions between counties, with rates ranging from 1,048.7 to 185.1 per 100,000. The highest rate of all admissions was seen in county Westmeath (1,048.7 per 100,000 total population), followed by Tipperary at 1,014.0 and Longford at 961.3. Monaghan had the lowest admission rate, at 185.1 per 100,000, followed by Cavan at 307.9 and Meath at 442.0. If one looks at two county services within the same health board, for example, Longford/Westmeath versus Laois/Offaly in the Midland Health Board, it is clearly seen that Longford/Westmeath has higher admission rates than the Laois/Offaly service, suggesting differing practice styles in service delivery in these services rather than any real difference in morbidity between these two areas. Likewise, it is interesting to note that all four counties in the North-Eastern Health Board (Cavan, Monaghan, Louth and Meath) accounted for the four lowest rates of all admissions, a factor reflecting the policy in that health board to treat persons with mental illness in the community.

First admission rates ranged from 285.9 per 100,000 in Westmeath to 52.6 in Monaghan. Waterford had the second highest rate, at 283.1, followed by Longford, at 271.8 per 100,000 total population. As with all admissions, the high first admission rate in both Westmeath and Longford was a factor in the overall high rate of admission in the Midland Health Board in 2001 (Daly & Walsh, 2003a) and the rates for these two counties were considerably greater than those for Laois/Offaly. Cavan had the second lowest rate of first admissions, at 113.3, followed by Limerick, at 124.8. Within the South-Eastern Health Board rates ranged from 136.7 per 100,000 for Kilkenny to 283.1 for Waterford, a two-fold difference in rates.

When diagnosis by county of residence was examined for all admissions in 2001 it was found that Longford had the highest rate for schizophrenia, at 295.0 per 100,000 total population, followed by Sligo at 265.1 and Tipperary at 192.5. The rate of admission for affective disorders was highest in Tipperary at 456.1, followed by Roscommon at 417.5 per 100,000.

Kerry had the highest rate of first admission for schizophrenia, at 48.4 per 100,000 total population, followed by Leitrim at 47.9 and Dublin at 46.9. Waterford had the highest rate of admission for affective disorders, at 121.5, followed by Roscommon at 121.2 and Longford at 106.1 per 100,000 total population. Longford had the highest rate of admission for alcoholic disorders, at 92.8 per 100,000 total population, followed by Westmeath at 88.4 and Carlow at 79.3.

Table 3.16   All and first admissions by county of residence 2001. Numbers and rates per 100,000 total population.

	Numbers		Rates	
	All	First	All	First
Dublin	6,798	2,416	642.4	228.3
Kildare	748	251	554.1	185.9
Wicklow	748	226	728.5	220.1
Laois	356	87	672.4	164.3
Longford	290	82	961.3[H3]	271.8 [H3]
Offaly	464	110	784.9	186.1
Westmeath	664	181	1,048.7[H1]	285.9 [H1]
Clare	604	122	642.5	129.8
Limerick	897	206	543.5	124.8 [L3]
Tipperary	1,354	303	1,014.0[H2]	226.9
Cavan	163	60	307.9[L2]	113.3 [L2]
Louth	446	128	483.9	138.9
Meath	485	142	442.0[L3]	129.4
Monaghan	95	27	185.1[L1]	52.6 [L1]
Donegal	1,054	277	810.8	213.1
Leitrim	173	50	690.4	199.5
Sligo	509	109	911.8	195.3
Carlow	350	91	841.0	218.7
Kilkenny	489	103	649.1	136.7
Waterford	731	268	772.1	283.1 [H2]
Wexford	624	159	597.9	152.3
Cork	2,575	829	612.4	197.1
Kerry	928	276	735.7	218.8
Galway	1,620	415	857.8	219.7
Mayo	703	192	630.4	172.2
Roscommon	464	119	892.7	229.0

H1 Highest rate of admission; H2 Second highest rate of admission; H3 Third highest rate of admission.
L1 Lowest rate of admission; L2 Second lowest rate of admission; L3 Third lowest rate of admission.

Despite policy initiatives to treat alcoholic disorders in the community services, rates for all and first admission were still quite high for some services and individual counties, in particular, Longford/Westmeath, Donegal, Galway, Carlow and Wicklow. The high rates for all and first admissions for alcoholic disorders in Wicklow (233.7 and 72.1) are in contrast to the low rates for two neighbouring services Dublin (75.9 and 30.7) and Kildare (74.1 and 29.6). Even within the Carlow/Kilkenny service, differences in the rates for alcoholic disorders are evident between the two counties, with Carlow having the higher rate for both all and first admissions. These high rates for Carlow are complemented by similarly high rates for that county relative to others in a recent study of community based treatment rates for problem alcohol use in the South Eastern Health Board (Drug Misuse Research Division, Occasional Paper No. 10, 2004). Within the North-Eastern Health Board there were also differences evident between the Cavan/Monaghan and Louth/Meath services for all disorders, with Cavan/Monaghan having lower rates in all cases.

Public versus private care

Our rates for health boards and counties have used as denominators the entire populations of these jurisdictions – those with medical cards and those covered by private health insurance. On the assumption that private medical insurance holders will be admitted to private hospitals and medical cardholders to health board institutions, it is possible – and more appropriate – to calculate rates of admission to both hospital types on the basis of their respective denominator populations; this has been done in this report.

The eligible medical card population as at September 2002 was extrapolated from the total population and has been employed as the denominator for calculation of public service rates. In addition, this population has been subtracted from the total to calculate rates for the totality of private hospitals. This has been done for all admissions and for first admissions and for the major diagnostic groups. It must be borne in mind that this is, at best, a crude differentiation between the two populations and hospital groups and makes a number of assumptions in its clear distinction between public and private populations. For instance, it is likely that some long-standing and enduring illness in the private insurance sector may run out of funding from that source and receive care from the public services; currently there is no means of knowing the extent of this and other occurrences (such as the unlikely scenario where medical card holders might be treated in private hospitals) likely to impact on the accuracy of the division and the consequent assumptions. Nevertheless the merit of this approach is that it does provide a more realistic basis for calculating rates from a more accurate population base than using total population figures.

Table 3.17   All and first admissions for selected diagnoses by county of residence 2001. Rates per 100,000 total population.

	All			First		
	Schizophrenia	Affective Disorders	Alcoholic Disorders	Schizophrenia	Affective Disorders	Alcoholic Disorders
Dublin	147.7	276.6	75.9	46.9	91.9	30.7
Kildare	141.5	279.3	74.1	33.3	94.1	29.6
Wicklow	155.8	216.2	233.7	29.2	68.2	72.1
Laois	105.8	258.8	190.8	11.3	68.0	39.7
Longford	295.0	321.6	265.2	46.4	106.1	92.8
Offaly	148.9	309.6	206.4	15.2	96.4	45.7
Westmeath	180.1	347.5	262.2	28.4	94.8	88.4
Clare	136.2	223.4	168.1	27.7	40.4	40.4
Limerick	113.9	222.4	78.8	18.2	46.7	21.2
Tipperary	192.5	456.1	221.7	20.2	100.3	52.4
Cavan	86.9	122.8	35.9	22.7	39.7	17.0
Louth	96.6	220.3	81.4	11.9	72.7	20.6
Meath	106.6	213.2	42.8	15.5	69.3	15.5
Monaghan	35.1	74.1	25.3	1.9	19.5	13.6
Donegal	163.9	328.5	232.3	30.8	80.0	73.8
Leitrim	155.6	231.5	127.7	47.9	67.8	27.9
Sligo	265.1	295.6	155.9	35.8	66.3	35.8
Carlow	165.8	242.7	252.3	12.0	64.9	79.3
Kilkenny	102.2	261.5	132.7	15.9	50.4	31.9
Waterford	133.1	363.3	132.0	44.4	121.5	65.5
Wexford	110.2	240.5	107.3	19.2	70.9	26.8
Cork	105.1	367.6	68.0	24.3	112.0	28.1
Kerry	185.5	273.5	140.3	48.4	72.1	42.8
Galway	191.2	343.7	204.4	25.4	91.1	70.4
Mayo	104.9	323.7	143.5	22.4	79.8	46.6
Roscommon	153.9	417.5	221.3	11.5	121.2	67.3

Table 3.18 presents all and first admission rates by health board in 2001 for the medical card populations of each board.

Table 3.18   All and first admissions to health board hospitals and units 2001. Rates per 100,000 eligible medical card population.[a]

	All		First	
	Numbers	Rates	Numbers	Rates
ERHA	6,186	1,746.4	2,092	590.6
Midland Health Board	1,606	2,224.0	378	523.5
Mid-Western Health Board	1,851	1,778.5	388	372.8
North-Eastern Health Board	970	894.6	257	237.0
North-Western Health Board	1,637	1,646.0	390	392.1
South-Eastern Health Board	2,838	2,005.9	722	510.3
Southern Health Board	3,331	1,845.5	1,009	559.0
Western Health Board	2,634	1,856.2	646	455.2
Total	21,053	1,751.1	5,882	489.2

aThe population figures are taken from the 2002 census of population (preliminary).

By reference to Table 3.16 and Table 3.13 it can be seen that, while the overall rates increase considerably over those based on total population, the relative rank-ordering remains much the same, although the rates for the ERHA have increased considerably and the North-Eastern Health Board retains its supremacy at the lowest rate.

Table 3.19 shows all and first admission rates by county for the medical card population, and should be compared with Table 3.17 for the same information for the total population. Again no great changes in rank order are apparent.

Table 3.19 All and first admissions to health board hospitals and units by county 2001. Rates per 100,000 eligible medical card population.[a]

	All		First	
	Numbers	Rates	Numbers	Rates
Dublin	4,952	1,732.6	1,742	609.5
Kildare	580	1,493.6	164	422.3
Wicklow	654	2,210.9	187	632.2
Laois	322	1,757.7	69	376.7
Longford	268	2,109.6	71	558.9
Offaly	427	2,170.0	93	472.6
Westmeath	590	2,742.8	145	674.1
Clare	559	1,768.1	103	325.8
Limerick	830	1,581.9	179	341.1
Tipperary	1,252	2,559.1	262	535.5
Cavan	142	720.8	52	264.0
Louth	379	973.6	95	244.0
Meath	375	1,181.2	92	289.8
Monaghan	74	409.8	18	99.7
Donegal	1,015	1,504.2	255	377.9
Leitrim	151	1,284.7	42	357.3
Sligo	475	2,348.8	93	459.9
Carlow	316	1,926.9	78	475.6
Kilkenny	452	2,204.2	91	443.8
Waterford	709	1,976.2	260	724.7
Wexford	565	1,420.7	136	342.0
Cork	2,443	1,796.5	754	554.5
Kerry	888	1,995.2	255	573.0
Galway	1,537	2,190.2	371	528.7
Mayo	661	1,297.8	167	327.9
Roscommon	437	2,101.4	109	524.1

a The population figures are taken from the 2002 census of population (preliminary).

Table 3.20 and Table 3.21 present all and first admission rates for the private population bases for the health board areas and counties in which persons admitted resided and it can readily be seen how much lower these are than those for the public sector (Table 3.18 and Table 3.19).

In Table 3.21 admission rates for the private sector by county are presented, with the comparison table again being Table 3.19. The differences are little short of astounding.

Table 3.22 and Table 3.23 present all and first admission rates by diagnosis for the public and private sectors.

Table 3.20 All and first admissions to private hospitals by health board of residence 2001. Rates per 100,000 private patient population.[a]

	All		First	
	Numbers	Rates	Numbers	Rates
ERHA	2,108	201.3	800	76.4
Midland Health Board	167	108.9	82	53.5
Mid-Western Health Board	166	70.4	71	30.1
North-Eastern Health Board	219	92.6	100	42.3
North-Western Health Board	95	77.9	46	37.7
South-Eastern Health Board	200	70.9	72	25.5
Southern Health Board	172	43.0	96	24.0
Western Health Board	152	63.8	79	33.2
Total	3,279	120.8	146	49.6

a The population figures are taken from the 2002 census of population (preliminary).
The denominator population was calculated by subtracting the eligible medical population from the total population.

Table 3.21 All and first admissions to private hospitals by county 2001. Rates per 100,000 private patient population.[a]

	All		First	
	Numbers	Rates	Numbers	Rates
Dublin	1,846	220.6	674	80.5
Kildare	168	134.2	87	69.5
Wicklow	94	110.4	39	45.8
Laois	34	84.1	18	44.5
Longford	22	119.4	11	59.7
Offaly	37	84.0	17	38.6
Westmeath	74	146.5	36	71.3
Clare	45	62.7	19	26.5
Limerick	67	54.4	27	21.9
Tipperary	102	111.6	41	44.9
Cavan	21	57.2	8	21.8
Louth	67	106.6	33	52.5
Meath	110	107.6	50	48.9
Monaghan	21	60.5	9	25.9
Donegal	39	55.8	22	31.5
Leitrim	22	156.5	8	56.9
Sligo	34	89.6	16	42.2
Carlow	34	115.5	13	44.1
Kilkenny	37	61.8	12	20.0
Waterford	22	33.5	8	12.2
Wexford	59	76.8	23	30.0
Cork	132	42.3	75	24.0
Kerry	40	45.5	21	23.9
Galway	83	59.9	44	31.7
Mayo	42	63.2	25	37.6
Roscommon	27	81.8	10	30.3

a The population figures are taken from the 2002 census of population (preliminary).
The denominator population was calculated by subtracting the eligible medical card population from the total population.

Table 3.22   All and first admissions by diagnosis to health board hospitals and units 2001. Rates per 100,000 eligible medical card population.[a]

	All		First	
	Numbers	Rates	Numbers	Rates
Organic Psychoses	547	45.5	172	14.3
Schizophrenia	4,528	376.6	918	76.4
Other Psychoses	299	24.9	140	11.6
Depressive Disorders	6,343	527.6	1,927	160.3
Mania	2,381	198.0	490	40.8
Neuroses	1,050	87.3	449	37.3
Personality Disorders	954	79.3	229	19.0
Alcoholic Disorders	3,750	311.9	1,124	93.5
Drug Dependence	701	58.3	275	22.9
Mental Handicap	290	24.1	42	3.5
Unspecified	292	24.3	167	13.9
Total	21,135	1,757.9	5,933	493.5

a The population figures are taken from the 2002 census of population (preliminary).

Table 3.23   All and first admissions by diagnosis to private hospitals 2001. Rates per 100,000 private patient population.[a]

	All		First	
	Numbers	Rates	Numbers	Rates
Organic Psychoses	130	4.8	66	2.4
Schizophrenia	286	10.5	71	2.6
Other Psychoses	34	1.3	23	0.8
Depressive Disorders	1,250	46.0	495	18.2
Mania	619	22.8	190	7.0
Neuroses	253	9.3	141	5.2
Personality Disorders	58	2.1	23	0.8
Alcoholic Disorders	616	22.7	323	11.9
Drug Dependence	43	1.6	28	1.0
Mental Handicap	5	0.2	2	0.1
Unspecified	17	0.6	6	0.2
Total	3,311	121.9	1,368	50.4

a The population figures are taken from the 2002 census of population (preliminary).
The denominator population was calculated by subtracting the eligible medical card population from the total population.

The following four tables present information on socio-economic group. In recent years returns to NPIRS on this parameter have deteriorated. For example, in 2001, 47% of occupations returned were unknown, thus making assignment to a socio-economic group impossible in these instances. We have thus used data for 1989, the last year when returns were near complete for this variable.

Of particular interest in Table 3.24 is the high rate of admission for farmers to health board hospitals and units for schizophrenia, depressive disorders and alcoholic disorders when compared with those of farmers admitted to private hospitals (Table 3.25). It is likely that farmers who have medical cards may tend to be smaller farmers and thus are quite a different group to those who are admitted to private hospitals. Among the unskilled group the high rate of admission to the public hospitals for alcoholic disorders (105.7), schizophrenia (90.2) and depressive disorders (88.4) is also striking and worth noting.

Table 3.24   All admissions to health board hospitals and units 1989. Socio-economic group by diagnosis. Rates per 100,000 eligible medical card population.[a]

	OrP	Sch	OP	DD	Man	Neur	PD	AD	DrDp	MH	Unsp
Farmers	9.1	48.0	1.0	73.4	27.9	9.7	5.3	39.3	0.7	3.1	3.2
Other Agricultural	1.8	18.8	0.3	13.7	4.2	1.4	3.0	12.1	0.6	1.0	1.0
Higher Professional	0.6	3.2	0.2	3.6	2.2	0.6	0.5	3.9	0.2	0.0	0.4
Lower Professional	1.6	13.9	0.4	13.8	7.6	2.9	1.4	10.4	0.5	1.2	1.1
Employers & Managers	0.2	1.4	0.2	2.5	1.4	1.0	0.5	3.2	0.1	0.2	0.6
Salaried Employees	0.2	2.5	0.2	4.9	2.0	0.8	0.5	3.8	0.1	0.0	0.2
Intermediate Non-Manual	5.9	44.5	1.3	50.4	18.4	10.6	11.4	53.1	1.5	1.8	4.6
Other Non-Manual	6.4	51.0	1.8	67.4	22.4	15.4	12.7	42.5	1.1	4.5	7.4
Skilled Manual	6.2	43.6	0.7	49.3	17.8	10.0	7.8	68.6	2.5	1.9	5.1
Semi-Skilled Manual	2.8	31.7	0.6	30.2	9.6	8.8	9.5	19.4	1.0	4.1	4.5
Unskilled Manual	11.5	90.2	1.9	88.4	24.5	16.2	21.5	105.7	3.7	7.8	7.6
Unspecified	10.7	94.0	2.4	63.9	28.6	15.8	27.2	60.9	2.6	10.2	12.5

a The population figures are taken from the 2002 census of population (preliminary).
OrP=Organic Psychoses Sch=Schizophrenia OP=Other Psychoses DD=Depressive Disorders Man=Mania Neur=Neuroses
PD=Personality Disorders AD=Alcoholic Disorders DrDp=Drug Dependence MH=Mental Handicap Unsp=Unspecified.

As can be seen from Table 3.24 and Table 3.25, the overall rate of admission to the private sector hospitals for all socio-economic groups is substantially lower than that to the public sector hospitals. The intermediate non-manual group had the highest rate of admission to private hospitals for almost all disorders, with no apparent reason for this.

Table 3.25   All admissions to private hospitals 1989. Socio-economic group by diagnosis. Rates per 100,000 private patient population.[a]

	OrP	Sch	OP	DD	Man	Neur	PD	AD	DrDp	MH	Unsp
Farmers	0.2	1.3	0.0	1.3	3.4	0.1	0.0	3.2	0.0	0.0	0.0
Other Agricultural	0.0	0.1	0.0	0.1	0.4	0.0	0.0	1.2	0.0	0.0	0.0
Higher Professional	0.8	1.8	0.0	1.9	6.1	0.8	0.1	5.3	0.1	0.0	0.0
Lower Professional	0.9	2.9	0.0	2.1	6.6	1.4	0.4	5.1	0.0	0.0	0.1
Employers & Managers	0.3	0.6	0.0	0.8	5.3	1.0	0.0	6.3	0.0	0.0	0.1
Salaried Employees	0.2	1.3	0.0	0.7	2.0	0.6	0.1	2.5	0.0	0.0	0.0
Intermediate Non-Manual	2.3	5.1	0.0	4.9	10.3	1.9	0.7	11.5	0.0	0.0	0.1
Other Non-Manual	0.1	1.1	0.0	1.1	5.9	0.6	0.1	4.7	0.0	0.0	0.1
Skilled Manual	0.3	1.4	0.0	2.3	2.9	0.9	0.1	7.2	0.0	0.0	0.0
Semi-Skilled Manual	0.1	0.8	0.0	0.8	0.6	0.3	0.1	2.3	0.0	0.0	0.0
Unskilled Manual	0.2	1.0	0.0	0.6	0.7	0.3	0.3	4.2	0.0	0.0	0.1
Unspecified	0.4	3.8	0.0	0.9	13.7	1.4	1.0	3.2	0.1	0.4	0.0

a The population figures are taken from the 2002 census of population (preliminary).
The denominator population was calculated by subtracting the eligible medical card population from the total population.
OrP=Organic Psychoses Sch=Schizophrenia OP=Other Psychoses DD=Depressive Disorders Man=Mania Neur=Neuroses
PD=Personality Disorders AD=Alcoholic Disorders DrDp=Drug Dependence MH=Mental Handicap Unsp=Unspecified.

Table 3.26   First admissions to health board hospitals and units 1989. Socio-economic group by diagnosis. Rates per 100,000 eligible medical card population.[a]

	OrP	Sch	OP	DD	Man	Neur	PD	AD	DrDp	MH	Unsp
Farmers	3.6	8.3	0.5	16.0	4.1	3.7	1.5	9.5	0.2	0.6	1.2
Other Agricultural	0.9	3.6	0.1	3.7	0.7	0.7	0.9	4.5	0.2	0.2	0.4
Higher Professional	0.2	1.0	0.0	1.5	0.7	0.5	0.2	0.9	0.0	0.0	0.2
Lower Professional	0.8	2.6	0.2	4.5	2.4	1.4	0.5	3.7	0.1	0.4	0.3
Employers & Managers	0.1	0.6	0.1	1.2	0.3	0.3	0.2	1.4	0.0	0.0	0.2
Salaried Employees	0.0	0.5	0.1	1.5	0.7	0.3	0.2	1.4	0.1	0.0	0.0
Intermediate Non-Manual	3.7	8.4	0.3	16.6	3.6	4.6	3.3	18.7	0.6	0.5	1.1
Other Non-Manual	2.7	7.0	0.8	16.5	3.3	4.9	2.4	13.6	0.6	0.3	1.4
Skilled Manual	2.6	7.1	0.2	16.6	4.1	3.9	3.2	25.1	0.8	0.2	1.8
Semi-Skilled Manual	1.0	5.0	0.1	8.8	1.2	2.1	2.5	7.2	0.4	0.2	1.4
Unskilled Manual	5.3	12.2	0.4	22.4	3.8	5.3	4.2	27.7	1.3	1.5	2.3
Unspecified	5.6	18.9	0.9	18.6	5.5	5.8	7.4	22.8	1.1	1.4	4.2

a The population figures are taken from the 2002 census of population (preliminary).
OrP=Organic Psychoses Sch=Schizophrenia OP=Other Psychoses DD=Depressive Disorders Man=Mania Neur=Neuroses
PD=Personality Disorders AD=Alcoholic Disorders DrDp=Drug Dependence MH=Mental Handicap Unsp=Unspecified.

As can be seen in Table 3.26 and Table 3.27 rates for first admission to the public sector hospitals were considerably higher than those to the private sector. Rates of first admission to public hospitals for the non-manual groups (intermediate non-manual and Other non-manual), the skilled and unskilled manual groups were substantially higher for depressive disorders and alcoholic disorders compared to rates for all other disorders among the other socio-economic groups.

Table 3.27 First admissions to private hospitals 1989. Socio-economic group by diagnosis. Rates per 100,000 private patient population.[a]

	OrP	Sch	OP	DD	Man	Neur	PD	AD	DrDp	MH	Unsp
Farmers	0.2	0.3	0.0	0.3	1.1	0.1	0.0	1.4	0.0	0.0	0.0
Other Agricultural	0.0	0.0	0.0	0.0	0.1	0.0	0.0	0.4	0.0	0.0	0.0
Higher Professional	0.4	0.4	0.0	0.9	1.5	0.5	0.0	2.1	0.0	0.0	0.0
Lower Professional	0.6	0.6	0.0	0.9	2.4	0.8	0.2	2.0	0.0	0.0	0.0
Employers & Managers	0.1	0.2	0.0	0.4	1.8	0.5	0.0	2.8	0.0	0.0	0.0
Salaried Employees	0.0	0.4	0.0	0.2	0.7	0.5	0.1	1.0	0.0	0.0	0.0
Intermediate Non-Manual	1.0	1.2	0.0	2.0	3.2	1.1	0.4	4.0	0.0	0.0	0.0
Other Non-Manual	0.0	0.2	0.0	0.3	2.0	0.3	0.0	1.6	0.0	0.0	0.0
Skilled Manual	0.1	0.5	0.0	0.7	0.8	0.6	0.0	3.4	0.0	0.0	0.0
Semi-Skilled Manual	0.1	0.1	0.0	0.2	0.1	0.2	0.0	1.1	0.0	0.0	0.0
Unskilled Manual	0.0	0.1	0.0	0.1	0.2	0.2	0.2	1.7	0.0	0.0	0.0
Unspecified	0.2	1.3	0.0	0.6	3.3	0.7	0.6	1.2	0.1	0.2	0.0

a The population figures are taken from the 2002 census of population (preliminary).
The denominator population was calculated by subtracting the eligible medical card population from the total population.
OrP=Organic Psychoses Sch=Schizophrenia OP=Other Psychoses DD=Depressive Disorders Man=Mania Neur=Neuroses
PD=Personality Disorders AD=Alcoholic Disorders DrDp=Drug Dependence MH=Mental Handicap Unsp=Unspecified.

Table 3.28 All and first admissions to public and private hospitals by legal status 2001. Rates per 100,000 medical card population (public) and private patient population.[a]

	All		First	
	Voluntary	Non-voluntary	Voluntary	Non-voluntary
Health board hospitals & units	1,546.7	211.2	424.8	68.7
Private hospitals	117.2	4.7	48.2	2.1

a The population figures are taken from the 2002 census of population (preliminary).
The denominator population for the private hospitals was calculated by subtracting the eligible medical card population from the total population

Table 3.29 Non-voluntary all and first admissions by socio-economic group 2001. Rates per 100,000 medical card (public) population and private patient population.[a]

	All			First		
	Health board hospitals & units	Private hospitals	Total	Health board hospitals & units	Private hospitals	Total
Farmers	12.1	0.1	3.8	3.5	0.0	1.1
Agricultural Workers	2.2	0.0	0.7	0.3	0.0	0.1
Higher Professional	2.9	0.4	1.2	0.8	0.1	0.4
Lower Professional	10.5	0.8	3.8	3.3	0.5	1.4
Employers & Managers	3.2	0.1	1.0	1.2	0.0	0.4
Own Account Workers	1.4	0.0	0.5	0.6	0.0	0.2
Non-manual	23.2	0.7	7.6	6.7	0.3	2.3
Manual Skilled	18.0	0.2	5.7	6.6	0.0	2.0
Semi-skilled	13.1	0.3	4.2	3.7	0.1	1.2
Unskilled	23.5	0.2	7.4	5.7	0.0	1.8
Unspecified	101.1	1.9	32.3	36.3	1.0	11.8
Total	211.2	4.7	68.1	68.7	2.1	22.6

a The population figures are taken from the 2002 census of population (preliminary).
The denominator population for the private hospitals was calculated by subtracting the eligible medical card population from the total population.

Table 3.29 presents non-voluntary all and first admission rates by socio-economic group for public versus private hospitals. The highest rate of non-voluntary admissions is seen among the non-manual group (for both all and first admissions) with far higher rates to the public sector than to the private. The same holds true for the manual skilled, semi-skilled, farmers and lower professionals.

These private/public comparisons are deeply revealing. Broadly, the public all admission rates are fifteen times and the first admission rates ten times those of the private sector and the ratio of first to all admission rates is much higher in the public service. The possible explanations are that there is far greater morbidity in the public sector, or that the private sector is therapeutically much more effective. Further exploration of these data and their explanations is clearly warranted. At the same time, the conclusion seems inevitable that the admission rates for the Irish public population must be among the highest anywhere. The differences in the certification (involuntary) rates of admission between the two sectors are very striking indeed

Discharges

In the face of a constant number of beds, equilibrium is maintained by the balance between those coming in and those going out. In other words, admissions must equal discharges and deaths. In the 19th century and early 20th century this balance was achieved by discharges, which amounted in the earlier years to half the numbers of admissions and by an equal number of deaths. For example, in 1923 there were 2,121 admissions, 1,362 discharges and 1,037 deaths; while in 1943 there were 2,036 admissions, 1,226 discharges and 1,170 deaths, little changes in the relative proportions in 20 years. By 1962, however, the scene had greatly changed, with 10,593 admissions, 9,906 discharges and 1,121 deaths, even though the number of deaths did not greatly differ from the earlier years. By 2002, however, deaths had become a trickle compared to admissions and to discharges (23,677 admissions, 23,716 discharges and 249 deaths). The greater mortality of the earlier years reflected the higher general population mortality as well as the proportionally greater mortality for those with psychiatric illness, which still persists.

In the nineteenth century the chances of discharge were small and one consequence was that first admissions predominated because to become a re-admission one had first to be a discharge. However, discharges did increase, although slowly at first, and, with them, re-admissions. Thus, in 1906 there were 555 re-admissions and by 1948, out of 2,788 total admissions, 978 were re-admissions. By 1960 re-admissions predominated and by the 1980's they formed three-quarters of all admissions.

The length of time discharges have spent in hospital has also reduced greatly. In 1923, of 1,005 discharges, 31 had spent less than one month in hospital; 267 between one and three months; a further 250 between three and six months; and a further 225 between six months and one year. After five years of hospitalisation the chances of discharge greatly diminished. Of those discharged in 1923 only 57 had been in hospital for that length of time. By 1943 the situation had changed little, of 982 discharges in that year, 13 had been hospitalised for less than one month, 190 for between one and three months, 276 between three and six months and a further 227 between six months and a year. In 2002, in contrast to the minuscule number discharged in under one month in both 1923 and 1943, 70% of the 26,000 discharges had been in hospital for less than one month. Curiously, the proportion discharged in under three months declined from 1923, when it was 30%, to 20% in 1943. By 2002 this figure was 90%.

CHAPTER 4

CHAPTER 4

The Waning of Confinement –
1960-2002

According to the *Commission of Inquiry on Mental Illness Report 1966* (Department of Health, 1966) there were 21,075 patients registered in psychiatric hospitals at the end of 1961, representing a hospitalisation rate of 7.3 per 1,000 population. This was reported as being possibly one of the highest rates of psychiatric hospitalisation at the time, especially when compared with rates of 4.5 in Northern Ireland, 4.6 in England and Wales, 4.3 in Scotland, 2.1 in France and 4.3 in the U.S.A. Such figures, along with an analysis of World Health Organisation (WHO) data around this time led to conclusions that Ireland had the 'highest rate of hospitalised morbidity in the world' (Walsh, 1968). Almost forty years later, a dramatic change in this hospitalised morbidity was evident.

By 1963, when the Commission of Inquiry on Mental Illness had conducted the first modern census of psychiatric residents, the 21,000 had fallen to 19,801. Table 4.1 monitors the continuing decline up to 2002. The residence figures in the table come from two sources: numbers for 1971, 1981, 1991 and 2001 come from the decennial censuses carried out by the MSRB and the HRB on the 31 March of each year, whereas the figures for the other years are those returned to the Department of Health on the 31 December when resident numbers are always lower than at any other time of the year. This explains why the 1971, 1981, 1991 and 2001 figures are all higher than the 1970, 1980, 1990 and 2000 numbers respectively. Otherwise, the only noteworthy feature of the table is the above-average drop of 1,600 between 1988 and 1989, largely due to the 'de-designation' of elderly and intellectually disabled patients in a small number of hospitals so that they were no longer classified as psychiatric residents. That the decline which we are describing has been the result of three main influences, deaths of hospital residents, mainly of older long-stay patients, their non-replacement by new long stay residents and shorter lengths of stay for recent patients, will be clear from the data that we are now presenting. The data presented in the following pages relate to the MSRB/HRB censuses carried out on 31 March in 1963 (Walsh, 1971), 1971 (O'Hare & Walsh, 1974b), 1981 (O'Hare & Walsh, 1983), 1991 (Moran & Walsh, 1992) and 2001 (Daly & Walsh, 2002).

There was an 80% reduction in the number of patients resident in psychiatric hospitals and units, from 19,801 in 1963 to 3,996 in 2002, and a 35% reduction in the ten-year period from 1992 to 2002 (Table 4.1).

Between 1965 and 2002, 28,439 patients died in psychiatric hospitals. Of those, 19,055 (68%) were over age 65 at death and 12,068 (42%) were old long-stay, that is, they had been over five years in hospital. Over the same time period an estimated 16,000 became new long-stay, being over one year in hospital without discharge.

A calculation of the mortality of the existing long-stay population of psychiatric hospitals and units of those aged over 65, of whom there were 1,396 in the public sector at the time of the Irish Psychiatric Hospitals and Units Census on the 31 March 2001, based on life tables, indicates that about two-thirds, 930, will have died

Table 4.1 Irish psychiatric in-patients 1963–2002. Numbers.

Year	Number	Year	Number	Year	Number	Year	Number
1963	19,801	1973	15,471	1983	12,802	1993	5,806
1964	18,989	1974	15,156	1984	12,484	1994	5,581
1965	18,641	1975	14,967	1985	12,097	1995	5,327
1966	18,084	1976	14,473	1986	11,643	1996	5,212
1967	17,841	1977	14,352	1987	10,621	1997	4,817
1968	17,218	1978	13,968	1988	9,500	1998	4,820
1969	16,802	1979	13,838	1989	7,897	1999	4,469
1970	16,403	1980	13,342	1990	7,334	2000	4,230
1971[a]	16,661	1981[a]	13,984	1991[a]	8,207	2001[a]	4,321
1972	15,856	1982	13,428	1992	6,130	2002	3,891

a MSRB/HRB Census completed on 31 March of each year (Walsh, 1971; O'Hare & Walsh, 1974b, 1983; Moran & Walsh, 1992; Daly & Walsh, 2002).

by 2011. The remaining 466 will die over the following years on a tailing-off basis, with some few survivors still remaining in the system by 2021. These projections over-estimate survival, based as they are on general population mortality experience, whereas there is well-documented evidence that psychiatric patients experience above-average mortality at all ages (Black *et al*, 1985; Harris *et al*, 1998; Ösby *et al*, 2001).

For those under 65, there are two issues to be considered – the decline of the long-stay population, that is those continuously hospitalised for more than one year on the 31 March 2001, of whom there were 2,166, and the numbers becoming new long-stay each year. Of the 2,166, 1,087 were over 65 and as they have already been accounted for in our earlier calculations we can exclude them from our further calculations. Thus, on the 31 March 2001 a total of 1,079 patients under 65 had been hospitalised for over one year continuously.

The *Activities of Irish Psychiatric Hospitals and Units 2002* (Daly & Walsh, 2003a) gives us information on the numbers leaving the long-stay population through discharge or death. These numbered 588 (276 under 65) in that year. Through the annual end of year returns to the Department of Health and Children we know that 81 persons under 65 became new long-stay in 2001. Therefore, the long-stay population under 65 is being depleted at a greater rate than it is being added to. On a very rough basis, and assuming that the 2001 numbers of removal from the long-stay population aged under-65 will continue at the same rate over ensuing years, that those under 65 becoming new long-stay will have the same removal characteristics as the existing under 65 long-stay population and that all long-stay patients have the same removal potential (that is that the ones leaving are not the 'easier', ones leaving a hard core, more difficult to discharge, residuum behind), then the under-65 long-stay population should have left hospital care by 2006.

The reduction in length of stay in hospital between 1965 and 2001 is presented in Table 4.2. Eight per cent of resident patients in 1971 had been hospitalised for less than one month, compared to 23% of patients in 2001. Likewise, the proportion of residents in hospital for 25 years and over has decreased from 20% in 1971 to 15% in 2001, despite increases in the intervening census years. It is interesting to note that 52% of these old long-stay residents in 2001 were over 65 years of age. The decrease in the proportion of old long-stay patients will continue with their deaths and their non-replacement by new long-stay patients. While the proportion of resident patients hospitalised continuously for one year or more has also declined, from 77% in 1971 to 54% in 2001, it still remains at over half of all residents.

Table 4.2   Irish Psychiatric Hospitals and Units Census 1963, 1971, 1981, 1991 and 2001. Length of stay. Numbers and percentages.

	Over 1 month	Over 3 months	Over 1 year	Over 5 years	Over 10 years	Over 25 years	All lengths of stay
				Numbers			
1963	-	17,639	-	11,992	-	-	19,801
1971	15,376	14,391	12,860	9,641	7,406	3,313	16,661
1981	12,511	11,626	10,502	8,089	6,372	2,913	13,984
1991	7,047	6,363	5,647	4,281	3,476	1,902	8,207
2001	3,328	2,735	2,316	1,538	1,170	630	4,321
				Percentages			
1963	-	89.1	-	60.6	-	-	100.0
1971	92.3	86.4	77.2	57.9	44.5	19.9	100.0
1981	89.5	83.1	75.1	57.8	45.6	20.8	100.0
1991	85.9	77.5	68.8	52.2	42.4	23.2	100.0
2001	77.0	63.3	53.6	35.6	27.1	14.6	100.0

Source: MSRB/HRB census completed on 31 March 1963, 1971, 1981, 1991 and 2001. (Walsh, 1971; O'Hare & Walsh, 1974b, 1983; Moran & Walsh, 1992; Daly & Walsh, 2002).

The proportion of old long-stay patients (i.e. those in hospital for five years or more) resident on each successive census night is presented in Figure 4.1. In 1963, almost two-thirds (61%) of residents had been in hospital for five years or more; in 2001 this proportion had decreased to 36%. The proportion in hospital for 25 years or more has not decreased greatly over the last almost 30 years, decreasing from 19.9% in 1971 to 14.6% in 2001 (Table 4.2).

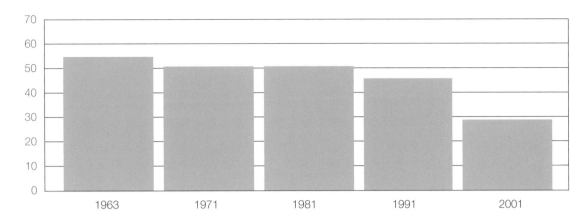

Figure 4.1 Irish Psychiatric Hospitals and Units Census 1963, 1971, 1981, 1991 and 2001. Percentage hospitalised for five years or more.

Source: MSRB/HRB census completed on 31 March 1963, 1971, 1981, 1991 and 2001. (Walsh, 1971; O'Hare & Walsh, 1974b, 1983; Moran & Walsh, 1992; Daly & Walsh, 2002)

Gender

The gender ratio of resident patients over the years has not changed significantly with males accounting for just over half of all residents in each census year (Table 4.3).

Table 4.3   Irish Psychiatric Hospitals and Units Census 1971, 1981, 1991 and 2001. Gender. Numbers and percentages.

	Males		Females		Total	Change	Change
						%	1963-1999 %
	Number	%	Number	%	Number		
1963	10,588	53.5	9,213	46.5	19,801		
1971	9,242	55.5	7,419	44.5	16,661	-15.9	
1981	7,737	55.3	6,247	44.7	13,984	-16.1	
1991	4,486	54.7	3,721	45.3	8,207	-41.3	
2001	2,395	55.4	1,926	44.6	4,321	-47.3	-78.1

Source: MSRB/HRB census completed on 31 March 1963, 1971, 1981, 1991 and 2001. (Walsh, 1971; O'Hare & Walsh, 1974b, 1983; Moran & Walsh, 1992; Daly & Walsh, 2002).

Age

Previous censuses have noted the fact that demographic characteristics, in particular age and marital status, are important factors in the high rate of hospitalised morbidity in Ireland (Walsh, 1971). Although absolute rates have fallen over the three census years, the trend in relation to age remains the same, with higher hospitalisation rates for the older age groups (Table 4.4). The hospitalisation rate for the 75-year and over group decreased from a rate of 1,735.7 in 1971 to 454.9 per 100,000 in 2001, the rate for the 65-74 year group decreased from 1,471.7 in 1971 to 345.5 per 100,00 in 2001 while that for the 55-64 year group decreased from 1,313.3 in 1971 to 256.7 per 100,000 in 2001. Hospitalisation rates for all age groups over 25 years decreased by almost half from 1991 to 2001, while the younger age groups had a less noticeable decline in rates.

Table 4.4   Irish Psychiatric Hospitals and Units Census 1971, 1981, 1991 and 2001. Age group.[a] Rates per 100,000 population.

	1971	1981	1991	2001[b]
Under 15 yrs	23.2	7.4	4.0	-[c]
15 – 19 yrs	108.7	46.0	31.7	32.9[d]
20 – 24 yrs	266.0	142.7	69.1	53.2
25 – 34 yrs	483.9	275.2	138.9	74.2
35 – 44 yrs	760.0	517.3	241.8	125.2
45 – 54 yrs	967.1	792.4	390.9	168.9
55 – 64 yrs	1,313.3	1,036.8	566.3	256.7
65 – 74 yrs	1,471.7	1,229.3	745.1	345.5
75 yrs & Over	1,735.7	1,608.6	1,048.9	454.9

Source: MSRB/HRB census completed on 31 March 1963, 1971, 1981, 1991 and 2001. (Walsh, 1971; O'Hare & Walsh, 1974b, 1983; Moran & Walsh, 1992; Daly & Walsh, 2002).
a Comparable rates for 1963 are not available.
b Rates per 100,000 population aged 16 years and over.
c Under 16 years.
d 16–19 years.

Socio-economic group

Other agricultural workers have had the highest rates of hospitalisation for each census year up to 2001, with rates in excess of 1,000 per 100,000 population in 1971 and 1981 (Table 4.5). The unskilled group had the highest rate in 2001, at 314.3 per 100,000. Employers and managers had the lowest rate of hospitalisation in 1963, 1981 and 1991, while own-account workers (self-employed without employees) had the lowest rate in 2001, at 5.8 per 100,000. Virtually all socio-economic groups had a reduction of over 66% in rates of hospitalisation from 1963 to 2001.

Table 4.5 Irish Psychiatric Hospitals and Units Census 1963, 1971, 1981, 1991 and 2001. Socio-economic group. Rates per 100,000 population.

	1963[a]	1971	1981	1991	2001[b]
Farmers	664	476.6	397.0	277.5	111.8
Other Agricultural/Agricultural Workers[b]	3,465	1,771.7	1,206.3	621.9	252.8
Higher Professional	736	450.8	276.0	109.7	49.9
Lower Professional	380	428.8	285.4	117.4	75.8
Employers & Managers	123	183.1	65.8	26.9	30.4
Salaried Employees/Own Account Workers[b]	144	179.6	175.2	83.8	5.8
Intermediate non-manual/Non-manual[b]	762	264.0	333.1	158.6	91.8
Other non-manual	481	932.2	651.2	279.4	
Skilled manual/Manual skilled[b]	508	218.5	160.7	77.3	61.0
Semi-skilled Manual	780	454.1	278.5	138.6	46.9
Unskilled Manual	944	617.2	838.9	583.5	314.3

Source: MSRB/HRB census completed on 31 March 1963, 1971, 1981, 1991 and 2001. (Walsh, 1971; O'Hare & Walsh, 1974b, 1983; Moran & Walsh, 1992; Daly & Walsh, 2002).
a Males only. Returns for females for 1963 were deemed to be unreliable.
b Revised CSO classification of occupations (Central Statistics Office, 1998).

Figure 4.2 illustrates the reduction in hospitalisation rates for selected socio-economic groups over each successive census. Other agricultural workers had the highest rate of hospitalisation for each census year up to 1991, with the unskilled group having the second highest. This pattern was reversed in the 2001 census, with the unskilled group having the highest rate. The hospitalisation rate for these two groups is compared with that of the lowest group for each census year, employers and managers.

Diagnosis

The diagnoses returned to the NPIRS are supplied by the clinicians in respect of their own patients in accordance with the edition of the International Classification of Diseases (ICD) prevailing and over the years moving from the eighth (WHO, 1974) to the tenth edition (WHO, 1992). Prior to the setting up of the NPIRS, the diagnoses used were those of the short list drawn up by the Commission of Inquiry on Mental Illness, consisting of 'schizophrenia' and 'depression' which were all inclusive and mutually exclusive. The changes in the ICD structures of these two diagnostic categories have been adjusted as follows to ensure that there is coherence in the diagnostic entities over the forty years.

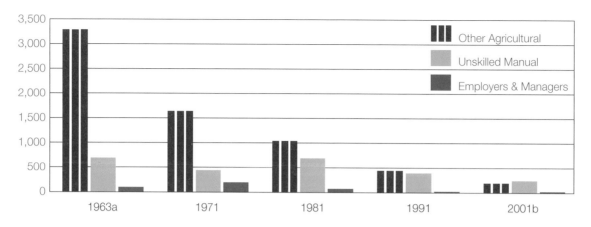

Figure 4.2 Irish Psychiatric Hospitals and Units Census 1963, 1971, 1981, 1991 and 2001. Selected socio-economic groups. Rates per 100,000 population.

Source: MSRB/HRB census completed on 31 March 1963, 1971, 1981, 1991 and 2001. (Walsh, 1971; O'Hare & Walsh, 1974b, 1983; Moran & Walsh, 1992; Daly & Walsh, 2002).
a Males only. Returns for females for 1963 were deemed to be unreliable.
b Revised CSO classification of occupations (Central Statistics Office, 1998).

For data from 1965–1969 the category 'schizophrenia' included schizophrenia (including 'paranoia' and 'paranoid psychosis') and 'schizophreniform', 'schizoaffective' or 'atypical' psychosis; from 1971 to 1980 the category included schizophrenia (ICD 8 numbers 295, 297 and Other and Unspecified Psychoses ICD 8 numbers 298 and 299); from 1980–1993 the ICD 9 (WHO, 1978) categories 'Schizophrenia' (295, 297, 298.3, 298.4) and 'Other and Unspecified Psychoses' (298.1, 298.2, 298.8, 298.9, 299) were included and from 1993 to the present the ICD 10 categories 'Schizophrenia' (F20, F21, F22, F23.1, F23.2, F23.3, F24, F25) and 'Other Psychoses' (F23.0, F23.8, F23.9, F28, F29, F53.1, F84) were used.

Due to our inability to access raw data for the years 1965–1969, the category 'depression' included 'manic-depressive psychosis' only instead of manic-depressive psychosis plus neurotic or reactive depression. From 1971–1980, depression included 'manic-depressive psychosis' (ICD 8 number 296) and neurotic depression (ICD 8 number 300.4); from 1981–1993 depression included 'depressive disorders' (ICD 9 numbers 296.1, 296.3, 298.0, 300.4, 309.0, 309.1, 311) and 'mania' (ICD 9 numbers 296.0, 296.2, 296.4, 296.5, 296.6, 296.8, 296.9).

Schizophrenia has consistently accounted for the highest proportion of the resident population in each successive census, although the proportion of residents has decreased from 53% in 1963 to 39% in 2001 (Table 4.6). The proportion of residents with depressive disorders increased slightly from 15% in 1991 to 17% in 2001, while the proportion with mania also increased slightly from 6% in 1991 to 10% in 2001. Despite the decrease in the proportion of residents with mental handicap/intellectual disability over successive years, due in part to the practice of de-designation, it still remains at 9% of the in-patient population.

Table 4.6 Irish Psychiatric Hospitals and Units Census 1963, 1971, 1981, 1991 and 2001. Diagnosis. Numbers and percentages.

	1963	%	1971	%	1981	%	1991	%	2001	%
Organic Psychoses	2,727	13.8	1,817	10.9	1,427	10.2	740	9.0	317	7.3
Schizophrenia	10,496	53.0	8,353	50.1	6,182	44.2	3,526	43.0	1,701	39.4
Other Psychoses	-	-	345	2.1	52	0.4	41	0.5	49	1.1
Manic-Depressive Psychosis	2,545	12.9	2,051	12.3	1,534	11.0	-	-	-	-
Depressive Disorders	-	-	-	-	-	-	1,202	14.6	752	17.4
Mania	-	-	-	-	-	-	481	5.9	424	9.8
Neuroses	968	4.9	555	3.3	798	5.7	422	5.1	146	3.4
Personality Disorders	306	1.5	218	1.3	296	2.1	374	4.6	125	2.9
Alcoholic Disorders	-	-	392	2.4	688	4.9	408	5.0	241	5.6
Drug Dependence	-	-	21	0.1	20	0.1	20	0.2	56	1.3
Mental Handicap	2,732	13.8	2,680	16.1	2,170	15.5	962	11.7	392	9.1
Unspecified	27	0.1	229	1.4	19	0.1	31	0.4	118	2.7
Total	19,801	100.0	16,661	100.0	13,984	100.0	8,207	100.0	4,321	100.0

Source: MSRB/HRB census completed on 31 March 1963, 1971, 1981, 1991 and 2001. (Walsh, 1971; O'Hare & Walsh, 1974b, 1983; Moran & Walsh, 1992; Daly & Walsh, 2002).

Figure 4.3 presents the change in hospitalisation rates from 1971 to 2001 for selected diagnostic groups. There was a 78% reduction in the hospitalisation rate for schizophrenia, with rates decreasing from 289.6 in 1971 to a rate of 63.1 per 100,000 in 2001. The rate of hospitalisation for mental handicap decreased by 84%, from 92.9 per 100,000 in 1971 to 14.5 in 2001.

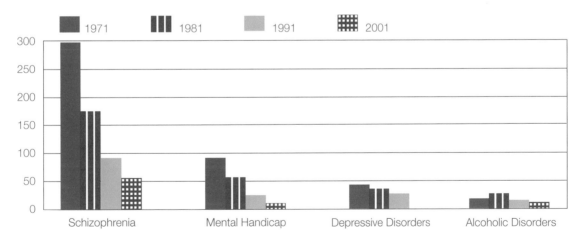

Figure 4.3 Irish Psychiatric Hospitals and Units Census 1971, 1981, 1991 and 2001. Change in hospialisation rate for selected diagnostic groups.

Source: MSRB/HRB census completed on 31 March 1963, 1971, 1981, 1991 and 2001. (Walsh, 1971; O'Hare & Walsh, 1974b, 1983; Moran & Walsh, 1992; Daly & Walsh, 2002).

Legal status

There was a very substantial reduction in the proportion of non-voluntary residents, from 78% in 1963 to 17% in 2001. Even in the ten-year period from 1991 to 2001, the proportion of non-voluntary residents decreased from 25% to 17%.

Health Board Areas

Health board areas had not been established in 1963, thus it is not possible to compare hospitalisation rates for all years. In 1971, 1981 and 2001, the Western Health Board had the highest rate of hospitalisation, followed by the Mid-Western and North-Western Health Boards (Table 4.7). In 2001 this pattern changed, whereby the South-Eastern Health Board had the highest rate.

Table 4.7   Irish Psychiatric Hospitals and Units Census 1971, 1981, 1991 and 2001. Health board areas. Rates per 100,000 population.

	1971	1981	1991	2001	% Decrease in rates 1971–2001
East Coast Area Health Board				105.0	
Northern Area Health Board				171.4	
South Western Area Health Board				99.1	
Eastern Health Board/ERHA	424.7	304.9	192.6	126.2	70.3
Midland Health Board	653.7	474.8	214.4	174.4	73.3
Mid-Western Health Board	685.4	530.5	268.2	220.7	67.8
North-Eastern Health Board	610.7	345.6	190.4	126.2	79.3
North-Western Health Board	685.4	544.0	172.0	100.9	85.3
South-Eastern Health Board	616.1	483.9	259.8	239.1	61.2
Southern Health Board	442.2	369.9	238.0	151.9	65.6
Western Health Board	912.7	615.3	372.1	214.4	76.5

Source: MSRB/HRB census completed on 31 March 1963, 1971, 1981, 1991 and 2001. (Walsh, 1971; O'Hare & Walsh, 1974b, 1983; Moran & Walsh, 1992; Daly & Walsh, 2002).

All health boards had a greater than 60% reduction in hospitalisation rates over the 30-year period 1971–2001. The North-Western Health Board had the largest percentage reduction in rates at 85%, followed by the North-Eastern Health Board with a 79% reduction and the Western Health Board, which had a 77% reduction in rates over this 30-year period. The South-Eastern Health Board had the smallest percentage reduction in rates over the same time period, at 61%.

Hospital type

There were nineteen general hospital psychiatric units in operation and reporting to the National Psychiatric In-patient Reporting System (NPIRS) in 2001. Seventy-two per cent of patients were resident in health board psychiatric hospitals in 2001, 14% were in general hospital psychiatric units and a further 14% were in private hospitals (Table 4.8). This represents a considerable increase in the proportion of residents in general hospital psychiatric units, from 3% in 1981 and 4% in 1991, resulting from an increase in the availability of such facilities over the years. The increase in residents in general hospital psychiatric units has seen a corresponding decrease in those resident in health board hospitals, from 95% in 1963 to 72% in 2001. There has also been an almost three-fold increase in the proportion of residents in private hospitals, from 5% in 1963 to 14% in 2001.

Table 4.8 Irish Psychiatric Hospitals and Units Census 1963, 1971, 1981, 1991 and 2001. Numbers and percentages.

	1963		1971		1981		1991		2001	
	Number	%	Number	%	Number	%	Number	%	Number	%
Health Board Hospitals	18,760	94.7	15,481	92.9	12,622	90.3	7,050	85.9	3,125	72.3
GH Units	0	0.0	149	0.9	376	2.7	362	4.4	614	14.2
Private Hospitals	1,041	5.3	1,031	6.2	986	7.1	795	9.7	582	13.5
Total	19,801	100.0	16,661	100.0	13,984	100.0	8,207	100.0	4,321	100.0

Source: MSRB/HRB census completed on 31 March 1963, 1971, 1981, 1991 and 2001. (Walsh, 1971; O'Hare & Walsh, 1974b, 1983; Moran & Walsh, 1992; Daly & Walsh, 2002).

Hospital beds

At the end of 2002 the total number of hospital beds was reported at 4,554 (Daly & Walsh, 2003b), representing a rate of 150.4 per 100,000 total population; the number of beds is higher than the number of patients because of less than 100% occupancy. Thus, the rate of beds per 1,000 population has declined in line with the declining hospitalised morbidity over the last forty years from a 'world high' of 7.3 in 1961 (Table 4.9). However, the rate in Ireland remains high by international standards according to a recent WHO report (WHO, 2001). The median number of beds per 10,000 population in Europe and North America is reported as 8.7 and 3.3 per 10,000 respectively. The UK rate is reported as 5.8 while that in the US is 9.5. The Irish rate was quite similar to that in France (12.0) but less than that of Canada, at 19.3 per 10,000. Table 4.9 presents the rates from this report, adjusted to the population per 1,000, along with rates for 1961 for various countries. Although there has been a dramatic reduction in the high rate of beds in Ireland at 7.3 in 1961 to 1.5 in 2002 this current rate is still one of the highest in the world along with that in the Netherlands (1.8), Denmark (1.5), Norway (1.3) and Canada (1.9).

Table 4.9   Psychiatric beds per 1,000 population 1961 and 2001. Ireland and selected countries.

Country	1961[a]	2001[b]
Ireland	7.3	1.5[c]
Northern Ireland	4.5	-
England and Wales	4.6	-
Scotland	4.3	-
UK	-	0.5
France	2.1	1.2
Spain	1.1	0.4
Portugal	0.9	0.7
Italy	2.2	0.1
Netherlands	2.3	1.8
Denmark	2.2	1.5
Belgium	3.1	2.5
Norway	2.9	1.3
Sweden	4.8	0.6
Finland	3.6	1.2
USA	4.3	0.9
New Zealand	3.5	1.3
Canada	3.9	1.9
Australia	3.1	0.4
Japan	1.1	2.8

a Source: Department of Health (1966) Commission of Inquiry on Mental Illness Report 1966. Dublin: Stationery Office.
b Source: WHO (2001) Atlas: Country Profiles of Mental Health Resources 2001. Geneva: WHO
c Source: Daly, A. & Walsh, D. (2003b) Activities of Irish Psychiatric Services 2001. Dublin: Health Research Board. The rates have been adjusted per 1,000 population.

The loss of 17,000 hospital beds or places has only been compensated for by the provision of about 3,000 community residential places. What has happened to the missing 14,000 former patients? In 1963 there were 2,732 mentally handicapped persons in psychiatric hospitals (Walsh, 1971); by 2001 there were 392 (Daly & Walsh, 2002). As with inpatients generally, the explanation was one of death and non-replacement. In this time period 1,911 died. Over the same time period, and reflecting policy change, the admission of such persons declined sharply from 563 in 1965 (O'Hare & Walsh, 1972) to 263 in 2002 (Daly & Walsh, 2003). Another factor determining the decline in the numbers of such persons in hospitals was the continuing policy of transferring those hospitalised to specialised facilities for the mentally handicapped and the de-designation of some parts of hospitals where they resided from that part of the hospital still dealing with psychiatric illness.

Also relevant to the issue of declining residence rates has been the decline in admission numbers and rates among the elderly as, with the growth of more specialised facilities for this age group, and particularly for those of them suffering from organic illness, dependence on the psychiatric hospital for 'catch-all' purposes, including the placement of the elderly, declined.

What other factors may have impacted on the decrease in residence rates? The establishment of community alternatives to in-patient treatment, such as day care, home care and other community-based interventions, will have helped to reduce admission rates and to shorten inpatient stay. With the further reduction in the old long-stay through mortality in this elderly population, inpatient requirements will fall further. While the addition of community alternatives has been a feature of services in recent years, the provision of these services has by no means reached an adequate level and much further progress in this area can be expected, with a corresponding further decline in inpatient requirements. Innovative methods of care delivery, community-based, such as the setting up of early intervention, crisis resolution/home care and assertive outreach teams, will work in the same direction, further reducing reliance on inpatient care. One final matter to be borne in mind is that the incidence of the most disabling illness of all, and the one making most demands on long-term residential care, schizophrenia, may be on the decline, an issue that we will return to in the next chapter. Even if this were not the case, the current policy of establishing specialised rehabilitation teams should reduce disablement from this disorder, again with lessened requirement for residential care.

CHAPTER 5

Summary and Conclusions

In the more modern literature there has been a body of opinion questioning whether there had not been an increase in major mental disorder around 1800 in view of the increased perception of the problem motivating the public legislative and service provision. Whereas there is ample evidence both from historical and literary sources that madness has been a component of the human condition since man has existed, the question was not whether insanity existed before the eighteenth century, but whether there had been an epidemic increase at that time or whether, like other disorders of decreasing virulence, such as scarlatina towards the end of the nineteenth century, but in the opposite direction, major mental disorder might have become a more malignant condition around 1800 (Cooper & Sartorius, 1977). Yet there are more parsimonious explanations which could be invoked. There appeared to be a contemporaneity in other population events, in Europe at least. Thus, there had been a population explosion in the eighteenth century, which was the consequence of improved life expectancy due to decreased mortality, particularly in early life. This was most often attributed to improved nutrition and increased resistance to the major causes of mortality such as cholera, smallpox, dysentery and tuberculosis. It would not be unreasonable to assume that mentally ill persons were disproportionately disadvantaged prior to the general betterment that accrued from improved conditions, including nutrition, and had higher mortality than the general population. They therefore, if this premise is correct, died early in life because of the handicaps of their mental illness. Accordingly, mental illness had low visibility and, by and large, was not viewed as a major community problem.

Another possible influence on the perceived increase was the shift in Western European populations as a whole, though admittedly less the case in Ireland, from an agricultural and rural-dwelling to an ever-expanding urban economy, with the increased burden which that imposed on family carers of the mentally ill as on those of the intellectually disabled and the elderly.

As to the nature of these illnesses which flooded into the nineteenth century asylums, some information was given in the Inspectors' reports of the nineteenth century. Terms such as melancholia, mania, monomania and alcoholic insanity were commonplace. While presumably melancholia equated with present-day depression, the precise entity of other conditions in terms of contemporary ICD or DSM nosology is unclear. Attempts, not entirely successful, have been made to convert the one to the other. These same reports did not flinch either from giving, in each individual case, the supposed cause of the illness – alcohol, snuff, or rather excess uses of them, being held responsible, in many instances, and in others, disappointment in love.

This publication has reviewed data sources relevant to mental illness in Ireland and attempted to elucidate from them matters relevant to the incidence and prevalence of psychiatric disorder and the consequences for service provision. The data presented derive almost uniquely from institutional or in-patient sources, although towards the end of the nineteenth century censuses of mentally ill persons in the community were being carried out by the Royal Irish Constabulary so as to determine the extent of further accommodation required to bring to finality the policy, enunciated many years before, of institutionalising all such persons in district asylums. While by 1900 this had been accomplished, with the result that one half per cent of the Irish population, almost 21,000 persons, was resident in the asylums, the twin objective of transferring such persons as still resided in workhouses would take much longer to bring about and was not a reality until well into the 20th century.

The incessant demand for ever-increasing places in asylums led to speculation in Ireland, as elsewhere, that the incidence of mental illness might be increasing. Many meetings and many papers were devoted to the topic and, at least in the early days of the controversy, the professional view was that insanity was definitely on the increase. The matter was of interest, not alone from the point of view of attempting to quantify the extent of further accommodation needed, but also to answer the more purely scientific question as to why there was this increase. Here in Ireland the matter was considered of such consequence that, as seen in chapter one, the Inspectors of Lunacy were requested to investigate the matter and determine whether the increase was apparent or real. This they did mostly by inviting the views of the medical superintendents throughout the country. Those who supported the real increase view sought explanations in the increased stress of modern life, tea-drinking, excessive use of alcohol and poor diet. On balance, though, opinion towards the close of the 19th century was that the apparent increase in insanity was due to 'accumulation' rather than to 'occurrence'.

No major changes occurred in the extent of our knowledge of changes in mental illness, its frequency, its causes, its treatment from 1900 to 1945, other than what was recounted in the routine annual reports of the Inspectors, now of Mental Hospitals rather than of Lunacy. These were generally years of depression, both economically and in cohesion of society, with a falling population, continuous emigration, low marriage rates and high incidence and mortality from tuberculosis. The generally poor conditions were reflected in a psychiatric system that was static if not stagnant. The difficulties, budgetary and otherwise, facing those striving for improvements were reflected in the comments of many frustrated service providers, even if consolation could be taken from the introduction of the Mental Treatment Act, 1945, making voluntary admission possible; slowly at first but increasingly over the ensuing years, this form of admission became more prevalent, as detailed in the reports.

The numbers in Irish mental hospitals continued to increase absolutely and in proportion to the population throughout the first half of the 20th century, reaching their apogee in 1958 at 21,000, the same number as for the 32 counties in 1900, and 0.7% of the population; there were, however, regional variations, with the figure for Sligo/Leitrim at 1.3%. These figures were so much higher than in other countries that they led to the setting-up of the Commission of Inquiry on Mental Illness in 1961. The Commission, reporting in 1966, deplored the almost exclusively institutional nature of psychiatric care, the fact that acute care was provided in mental hospitals rather than in general hospitals, the absence of child psychiatric services and of psychologists, social workers and occupational therapists in services and the lack of involvement of general practitioners in providing psychiatric care. On the issue as to whether there was, relative to neighbouring countries, more psychiatric illness in Ireland and, if so, of what type, they did not express an opinion, other than to say that that was a matter that should be investigated by the Medico-Social Research Board, with the results that have been presented earlier in this report.

We have seen the five-fold decline in the numbers of those hospitalised, from 21,000 in 1958 to 4,000 in 2001, and we have reviewed the reasons for this fall. Most of the decline has been shown to have been the consequence of mortality among the long-stay population and its non-replacement by greatly diminished accretion of new long-stay patients from among newer, younger inpatients. The growth of community residential care as an alternative to long-stay institutional care has played a significant role in this as well. This is exemplified by the fact that by 2001 there were over 3,000 community-based residential places provided by psychiatric services, as well as a smaller number by voluntary organisations. We have shown on the basis of life tables that, of the current 2,500 long-stay population the great majority of whom are elderly, two thirds will have died by 2011. Community resettlement of others if it were to happen, such as by transfer to nursing homes to cater for their increasing physical enfeeblement, would expedite even further the decrease of the long-stay psychiatrically institutionalised. This should, of course, be a major policy objective and any patients requiring continuing residential accommodation, whether because of homelessness or severity of impairment, whether functional or symptomatic, from residual illness, should find this care in community residential locations rather than in a hospital setting, whether provided by local housing authorities or by mental health services or voluntary agencies.

We have observed how the numbers and rates of admission soared from the 1950s to the 1980s and then stabilised and how the proportion of re-admissions climbed to constitute 75% of all admissions. First admissions also increased over this same period, though not at the same rate as re-admissions, and they, too, stabilised in the early 1980s. As in hospital residency rates, we have seen significant differences between services in admissions rates, which are more likely the consequence of differing service delivery styles than any regional discrepancies in disease incidence or prevalence. There are some quite interesting trends in admission rates over time for different diagnostic groups. For example, those for alcohol-related disorders have, not surprisingly, mirrored the increase in alcohol consumption nationally; a more recent decline reflects, in all likelihood the preferred policy option of treating alcohol dependence in specialised community-based settings, although the variations in admission rates between services reflects the reality that some have moved to this change earlier and more extensively than others.

The reduction in first admission rates for schizophrenia over the 40-year period is striking, almost 40%, and complements data from elsewhere (Eagles & Whalley, 1985) that hint that the incidence of this major disorder may be on the decline. Of course all studies do not confirm this trend (Boydell *et al*, 2003) and it has to be borne in mind that the traditional wisdom in relation to this condition – that it was of such social disruptiveness that ultimately all cases would be hospitalised at least once in their lifetime – may not now, in the face of more community-based treatment options, be valid. Nevertheless, from the point of view of our in-patient data there appears not to be a compensatory increase in other conditions were changes in diagnostic practises invoked as an explanation. However, the first admission data for this condition show considerable inter-county variation, over three-fold in some instances, and therefore far greater than the variation in first admission rates for all diagnoses combined. This supports the case for further examination of the matter on a case-by-case basis, with particular regard to the validity of the 'first' admission and diagnostic variables. Community-based examinations of schizophrenia incidence in Ireland have not indicated a raised frequency of the condition in this country (Ní Nualláin *et al,* 1987; Jablensky *et al,* 1997).

The extraordinary differences in admission rates between the private and public sectors as well as between socio-economic classes, which is independently apparent, point indubitably to poverty and disadvantage as being closely linked to both the incidence and prevalence of mental illness. It is also very relevant to our attempt to understand the 19th century phenomenon of pauper lunacy and the establishment of an asylum system side by side with the indoor poor relief mechanism for responding to it. Indeed, at first the asylum system was viewed as part of a wider welfare system for the indigent poor and was managed as such; it was only as the century wore on that lay managers were replaced by physicians and the medicalisation of lunacy began.

That the emigrant Irish in America were no less poor and lunatic than their fellows at home is clear from the fascinating review of lunacy in the Commonwealth of Massachusetts by Jarvis (1855). This, the first prevalence study of mental illness in the United States, was triggered by a protestant and humanitarian ethic to provide care for the indigenous population. However, as his work progressed Jarvis found that the resources of the State Hospital at Worcester and other facilities, not to speak of the community itself, were being overwhelmed by emigrant pauper Irish. Of the 625 foreign lunatics enumerated, 512 were Irish and 93% were paupers. 'The Irish labourers have less sensibility and fewer wants to be gratified than the Americans, and yet they more commonly fail to supply them. They also have a greater irritability: they are more readily disturbed when they find themselves at variance with the circumstances about them, and less easily reconciled to difficulties they cannot overcome. Unquestionably much of their insanity is due to their intemperance, to which the Irish seem to be particularly prone, and much to that exaltation which comes from increased prosperity.' Jarvis was much preoccupied by the link between poverty and lunacy and, in as far as he came to any conclusions on the matter, they were to the effect that the relationship was in large measure determined by inherent characteristics. An advocate of early intervention he believed that the Irish were inherently less likely to recover from mental illness once it struck. That the prominence of mental illness in the New World Irish was not to diminish for some further time was evident from studies of the turn-of-the-century Irish in the United States (Malzberg, 1936, 1963). However, as they assimilated and their indigence was replaced by rising prosperity, their high rates of hospitalised mental illness decreased as the years passed and they were replaced in the league table by newer, poorer immigrant groups, once again exemplifying the link with poverty, whatever the mediating social physical and biological mechanism might be. Similar data relating to the Irish in Britain, even into the first generation, have been noted (Dean *et al,* 1981; Harding & Balarajan, 1996) and it is not without import that newer, West Indian, African-Caribbean immigrants to that country have also been identified as being of greatly elevated risk for schizophrenia (Harrison *et al,* 1997). The complex interrelationships thus exemplified postulate genetic and, therefore biologic, vulnerability to serious mental disorder which exhibits itself in both pre-and post-illness social and educational disadvantage, particularly in the case of schizophrenia, which vulnerability is both an antecedent to and consequence of the disorder (Agerbo *et al.,*2004). Whereas the inverse relationship between social class and schizophrenia has been general (Goldberg and Morrison, 1963), there have been some dissenting findings. These include a recent Irish study in a somewhat, from the point of view of social composition, atypical catchment area (Mulvany *et al.,* 2001), and one in which schizophrenia incidence appears to have fallen considerably (O'Hare and Walsh, 1987; Daly and Walsh, 2003).

The lack of decline in affective disorders is consonant with the relatively poor long-term outcome of cohorts of depressed patients (Keller et al 1984; Kiloh et al 1988: Kanai et al 2003). That there has been no reduction co-incident with the introduction and proliferation of anti-depressant medication is noteworthy but not out of keeping with many reports failing to find a significant impact, at least from a public health point of view, of these medications (Moncrieff, 2003). Indeed if, as many clinicians claim, depression is the main factor in suicide, no solace can be found in the observation that, in Ireland, the rise of suicide (Table 5.1 and Table 5.1a) and the increase in the deployment of anti-depressant drugs have run in parallel. It has not been possible to obtain reliable information on the extent of prescribing of anti-depressant medication either as a total figure, or over the years, in Ireland, and so it is not possible to ascertain what the undoubted considerable increase has been.

In relation to the relationship between social-economic disadvantage and mental illness, the findings are unequivocal, at least from hospital data. For every condition, those in lower class positions are disadvantaged in residence and admission rates that are several times higher than for those in more privileged positions. Another area where there are anomalies between social groups and between the public service and private sectors is in the proportion of admissions that are involuntary and, within the public, there are inter-service differences of major proportions in a background of moderately high involuntary rates in European terms.

(Table 5.2). It should be remembered that as admission numbers diminish a bias towards more seriously ill patients only being admitted becomes apparent, with the likelihood that a greater proportion will therefore be involuntary.

Table 5.1   Suicide in Ireland for various years 1976–2002. Numbers and rates per 100,000 total population.

	Males		Females		Total	
	Numbers	Rates	Numbers	Rates	Numbers	Rates
1976	129	7.9	54	3.4	183	5.7
1980	143	8.4	73	4.3	216	6.4
1985	216	12.2	60	3.4	276	7.8
1990	251	14.4	83	4.7	334	9.5
1995	321	18.0	83	4.6	404	11.2
2000[a]	341	18.1	72	3.8	413	10.9
2002[a]	371	19.1	80	4.1	451	11.5

a These data relate to deaths registered in these years.

Table 5.2.   Involuntary admissions. Various European countries and years. Percentage of all admissions and rates per 100,000 population.

Country	Year	Percentage of all Admissions	Rate per 100,000 population
Austria	1999	18.0	175.0
Belgium	1998	5.8	47.0
Denmark	2000	4.6	34.0
Finland	2000	21.6	218.0
France	1999	12.5	11.0
Germany	2000	17.7	175.0
Ireland All	2001	11.4	69.4
Public	2001	13.0	211.2
Private	2001	3.0	4.7
Netherlands	1999	13.2	44.0
Portugal	2000	3.2	6.0
Sweden	1998	30.0	114.0
England	1999	13.5	48.0

Source; European Commission. Compulsory Admission and Involuntary Treatment of Mentally Ill Patients – Legislation and Practice in EU Member States (2002). Central Institute for Mental Health. Mannheim, Germany.

Data on expenditure on mental health services have been available from the nineteenth century, in fact more or less from the inception of the asylum system. In 1875 the non-capital cost was £197,417, which by 1989 had risen to £360,395, and by 1923 to £944,315. It has not proved possible to cost this expenditure as a proportion of all health expenditure for earlier years but, beginning with the financial year 1956/57, such comparisons become feasible. In that year, of a total non-capital health expenditure of just over £17,000,000, over £3,000,000 went to mental health services, a proportion of 19.5%, which by 1960/61 had reached 20.0%. By 1977 these figures had become £193,000,000 and £29,000,000 respectively – a drop to 15%.

More recently, expenditure on psychiatric service in absolute terms has increased from €196 million (converted from Irish Punts) in 1988 to €563 million in 2002, an increase of 187% as the following table shows.

Table 5.3   Expenditure on mental health services versus total health expenditure 1988–2002.

	Total health expenditure	Mental health expenditure	Mental health expenditure as % of total health expenditure
	€000m	€000m	
1988	1,564	196	12.5
1989	1,318	158	11.9
1990	1,464	168	11.4
1991	1,631	183	10.3
1992	1,830	197	10.8
1993	2,016	209	10.4
1994	2,145	216	10.1
1995	2,299	228	9.9
1996	2,354	232	9.8
1997	3,443	326	9.5
1998	3,819	347	9.1
1999	4,573	394	8.6
2000	5,354	433	8.1
2001	6,739	497	7.4
2002	8,166	563	6.9

Source: Health Statistics various years.

During the same time, such expenditure as a percentage of all health expenditure has almost halved, down from 12.5% in 1988 to 6.9 in 2002, a decline of 44.8 %, while in-patient numbers have fallen from 9,500 to 3,966, a decline of 58%. Community residential places have increased from 1,625 to 3,146 (Department of Health and Children, 2003b), an increase of 94%; consultant numbers have increased from 159 to 266 an increase of 67%; and the number of psychiatric nurses decreased from 6,229 to an estimated 5,223. In fact there has been an almost direct relationship between the proportional decline in spending and the fall in bed numbers.

It is worth recalling the decline in non-capital national expenditure on mental health services as a proportion of all health expenditure over the past 40 years from 21% in financial year 1960/61 – £4,000,000 out of £19,500,000 – to €196,000,00 (12.5%) out of €1,564,000,000 and €563 ,000,000 out of €8,166,000,000 or 6.9% in 2002. With over 80% of this expenditure being absorbed by wages and salaries, the greater part of it being to nursing staff, this decline has to be seen in the context of the greatly reduced in-patient base to be supported, by far the most costly component of any service, and reflected in the reduction of staff numbers required to service it on a 24-hour basis. For example, in 1904 there were 1,643 attendants in the service (for 32 counties); by 1923 this had increased to 2,102 and by 1940 to 2,540. In 1955 (by which time attendants had become nurses) there were 3,448 employed by 1970, 7,000 declining to 6,040 in 1982 and to 5,125 in 1988, with further declines in later years, although a small proportion were deployed in community-based activity. It has, for example, been estimated that in one of the most 'communitised' services in the country, with a minimal in-patient base, this small element still manages to consume 40% of revenue. It is striking how little concern there is to examine how cost-efficient and effective our current mental health spend really is.

Suspicions that in the comparative sense, we do not fare well in this regard may be raised by the consideration that in the United Kingdom the National Health Service expenditure on mental health services was 4.1 billion Pounds Sterling in 2002 (Appleby, 2003). Allowing for Euro conversion, this represents approximately €69 per head of population compared to €144 in Ireland for the same year. Furthermore, the inflation-adjusted expenditure increase from 1997 to 2002 in Ireland was 44% while that of the UK was just over 30%. It should be born in mind that as these figures are not age adjusted and take no account of the substantial private sector mental health expenditure in Ireland, the situation is even less favourable than the crude figures portray. The inevitable conclusion must be that we in Ireland get poorer value for our money. Why this should be so requires in-depth exploration. Here it is appropriate to return to our point of departure and point out that, even if questions concerning the niceties of expenditure were asked, there would be little information on which to make judgement, given the poor state of budgetary information available to us. Nonetheless, whatever about revenue, the case for increased capital support for mental health services is strong, to complete the general hospital psychiatric unit building programme and to provide further community-based residential accommodation. In recent years the capital health spend has never exceeded

5% of all health spend and has dipped below 2% on occasion. The proportion of capital spend on mental health services, of the total capital spend, has fluctuated from 2.0% in 1997 (the most usual figure) to the unusually higher 5.7% in 2000.

Overall, our inpatient reporting system has served us well and has yielded useful information for scientific and planning purposes. Yet significant problems remain. Recent years have seen a deterioration in the reporting of socio-economic status due to difficulties in having services return occupational details, with a decline in the number of cases in which this information is supplied, from almost complete coverage in the mid-and late-1970's, to 47% more recently. We are aware that in most services there is little by way of formal incentives, or indeed mechanisms, in place for collecting information; for instance there are no ward clerks in almost all services and the data collection function is, in most cases, an additional rather than a core task for staff in health boards returning information. The HRB, however, has now taken an initiative in this matter by organising formal training on a regional basis for those tasked with making returns to the NIPRS. Another difficulty has been the acquisition of diagnoses. There has been a remarkable and troublesome reluctance on the part of psychiatrists to supply ICD diagnoses to the system, which has proved most intractable and does not flatter current training programmes for psychiatric medical trainees.

Finally, inpatient data tell only some of the story. Cognisant of this a three county case register to register was set up to register every contact with the specialist psychiatric services in tandem with a similar case register in the Dublin South West psychiatric service in those counties. This initiative was used for planning and scientific purposes in conjunction with many studies, our own and others, but more recently had been experiencing operational difficulties and has been closed down. It is important that this type of vital information gathered by the Psychiatric Case Register is available in the future for the rational planning of services. Thus, the Mental Health Research Division of the HRB has developed a software system aimed at capturing the activities of community psychiatric services called, COMCAR. This system will be piloted in 2004 with a view to rolling it out nationally following evaluation.

The lack of any community-based survey of psychiatric morbidity in this country, apart from some local assessments, notably of the elderly (Lawlor, 1994), such as have been carried in other jurisdictions – by the DHSS in the UK (Meltzer *et al,* 1995) and the Epidemiological Catchment Area (ECA) study in the US (Reiger *et al,* 1984) – limit our capacity to plan rationally our services of the future. Whether sufficient resources will become available to undertake such undoubtedly costly surveys and studies remains to be seen.

REFERENCES

Appleby L (2003) So, are things getting better? *Psychiatric Bulletin,* 27, 441-442.

Agerbo E, Byrne M, Eaton W & Mortensen PB (2004). Marital and Labor Market Status in the Long Run in Schizophrenia. *Archives of General Psychiatry,* 61 (1) ; 28 – 33.

Black DW, Warrack G & Winokur G (1985) Excess mortality among psychiatric patients. The Iowa Record-Linkage Study. *Journal of the American Medical Association,* 253, pp. 58-61.

Boydell J, van Os, J, Lambri M, Castle D, Allardyce J, McCreadie RG & Murray RM (2003) Incidence of schizophrenia in south-east London between 1965 and 1997. *British Journal of Psychiatry,* 182, pp. 45-49.

Central Statistics Office (1998) *Ireland. Census '96: Principal Socio-economic Results.* Dublin: Stationery Office.

Cooper J & Sartorius N (1977) Cultural and temporal variations in schizophrenia: a speculation on the importance of industrialization. *British Journal of Psychiatry,* 130, pp. 50-55.

Daly A & Walsh D (2002) *Irish Psychiatric Hospitals and Units Census 2001.* Dublin: Health Research Board.

Daly A & Walsh D (2003a) *Activities of Irish Psychiatric Services 2001.* Dublin: Health Research Board.

Daly A & Walsh D (2003b) *Activities of Irish Psychiatric Services 2002.* Dublin: Health Research Board.

Dawson WR (1911) The Presidential address on the relation between the geographical distribution of insanity and that of certain social and other conditions in Ireland. *Journal of Mental Science,* 57, pp. 571-597.

Dean G, Downing H, Shelley E (1981) First admissions to psychiatric hospitals in south-east England in 1976 among immigrants from Ireland. *British Medical Journal* (Clin Res Ed), 282(279), pp. 1831-1833.

Department of Health (Various years) *Reports of the Inspector of Mental Hospitals.* Dublin: Stationery Office.

Department of Health (1966) *Commission of Inquiry on Mental Illness 1966 Report.* Dublin: Stationery Office.

Department of Health (1984) *The Psychiatric Services – Planning for the Future.* Dublin: Stationery Office.

Department of Health and Children (2001) *Quality and Fairness. A Health System for You. Health Strategy.* Dublin: Stationery Office.

Department of Health and Children (2003a) *Health Statistics 2002.* Dublin: Stationery Office.

Department of Health and Children (2003b) *Report of the Inspector of Mental Hospitals for the year ending 2002.* Dublin: Stationery Office.

Drapes T (1894) On the alleged increase of insanity in Ireland. *Journal of Mental Science,* 40, pp. 519-548.

Drug Misuse Research Division (2004) *Occasional Paper No. 10.* Dublin: Health Research Board

Eagles JM & Whalley LJ (1985) Decline in the diagnosis of schizophrenia among first admissions to Scottish Mental Hospitals from 1969-78. *British Journal of Psychiatry,* 146, pp. 151-154.

Finnane M (1981) *Insanity and the Insane in Post-famine Ireland.* London: Croom Helm

Foucault M (2001) *Madness and Civilization.* London and New York: Routledge Classics

Barron S & Mulvany F (2003) *Annual Report of the National Disability Database.* Dublin: Health Research Board

Goldberg FM and Morrison SL (1963). Schizophrenia and Social Class. *British Journal of Psychiatry,* 109; 785–802.

Grob G in Jarvis J (1971) *Insanity and Idiocy in Massachusetts: Report of the Commission on Lunacy, 1855.* University Press, Cambridge, Massachusetts.

Jablensky A (1997) The 100-year epidemiology of schizophrenia. *Schizophrenia Research,* 28, pp. 111-125.

Jarvis E (1855). Report on Insanity and Idiocy in Massachusetts, by the Commission on Lunacy. Boston, William White.

Jones K (1960) Mental Health and Social Policy 1845 – 1959. London: Routledge and Keegan Paul.

Harding S & Balarajan R (1996) Patterns of mortality in second generation Irish living in England and Wales: longitudinal study. *British Medical Journal,* 312(7043), pp. 1389-1392.

Harris EC & Barraclough B (1998) Excess mortality of mental disorders. *British Journal of Psychiatry,* 173, pp. 11-53.

Harrison G, Galzebrook C, Brewin J, Cantwell R, Dalkin T, Fox R, Jones P & Medley I (1997) Increased incidence of psychotic disorders in migrants from the Caribbean to the United Kingdom. *Psychological Medicine,* 27(4), pp. 799-806.

Kanai T, Takeuchi H, Furukawa TA, Yoshimura R, Imaizumi T, Kitamura T & Takahashi K (2003) Time to recurrence after recovery from major depressive episodes and its predictors. *Psychological Medicine,* 33, pp. 839-845.

Keller MB, Klerman GL, Lavori PW, Coryell W, Endicott J & Taylor J (1984) Long-term outcome of episodes of major depression: clinical and public health significance. *Journal of the American Medical Association,* 252, pp. 788-792.

Kennedy N, Abbott R & Paykel ES (2003) Remission and recurrence of depression in the maintenance era: long-term outcome in a Cambridge cohort. *Psychological Medicine,* 33, pp. 827-838.

Kiloh LG, Andrews G & Nielson M (1988) The long-term outcome of depressive illness. *British Journal of Psychiatry,* 153, pp. 752-757.

Lawlor B, Radic A, Bruce I *et al* (1994) Prevalence of mental illness in the community-dwelling elderly in Dublin using AGECAT. *Irish Journal of Psychological Medicine,* 11, pp. 157-160.

MacAlpine I (1992) *George III & The Mad Business.* London: Surveillance Books.

Malzberg B (1936) A statistical study of mental diseases among natives of foreign white parentage in New York State. *Psychiatric Quarterly,* 10, pp. 127-142.

Malzberg B (1963) Mental disease among Irish born and native whites of Irish parentage in New York State 1949-1951. *Mental Hygiene,* 47, pp. 12-42.

Meltzer H, Gill B, Petticrew M & Hinds K (1995) *OPCS Surveys of Psychiatric Morbidity in Great Britain. Report 1. The prevalence of psychiatry morbidity among adults living in private households.* London: HMSO.

Mental Treatment Act (1945).

Moncrieff J (2003) Antidepressant prescribing and suicide. *British Medical Journal,* 327, pp. 288.

Moran R & Walsh D (1992) *The Irish Psychiatric hospitals and Units Census 1991.* Dublin: Health Research Board.

Mulvany F, O'Callaghan E, Takei N, Byrne M, Fearon P & Larkin C (2001) Effect of Social Class at Birth on Risk and Presentation of Schizophrenia; Case-control Study. *British Medical Journal.* 323 (7326): 1389–1401.

National Suicide Review Group (1999) *Annual Report 1999.*

National Suicide Review Group (2001) *Annual Report 2001. Suicide Prevention Across the Regions.*

Ní Nualláin M, O'Hare A & Walsh D (1987) Incidence of schizophrenia in Ireland. *Psychological Medicine,* 17, pp. 943-948.

Nugent J (1858) *Observations on the report of the commissioners of inquiry into lunatic asylums (Ireland).* Dublin: Alex Thom and Sons.

O'Dwyer F (1997) *Irish Hospital Architecture.* Dublin: Department of Health and Children.

O'Hare A & Walsh D (1972) *Activities of Irish Psychiatric Hospitals and Units 1965–1969.* Dublin: Medico-Social Research Board.

O'Hare A & Walsh D (1974a) *Activities of Irish Psychiatric Hospitals and Units 1970.* Dublin: Medico-Social Research Board.

O'Hare A & Walsh D (1974b) *The Irish Psychiatric Hospital Census 1971.* Dublin: Medico-Social Research Board.

O'Hare A & Walsh D (1983) *The Irish Psychiatric Hospitals and Units Census 1981.* Dublin: Medico-Social Research Board.

O'Hare A and Walsh D (1987). *Activities of Irish Psychiatric Hospitals.* Dublin: Health Research Board.

Ösby U, Brandt L, Correia N, Ekbom A, Sparén P (2001) Excess mortality in bipolar and unipolar disorder in Sweden. *Archives of General Psychiatry,* 58, pp. 844-850.

Reiger DA, Myers JK, Kramer M, Robins LN, Blazer DG, Hough RL, Eaton WW & Locke BZ (1984) The NIMH Epidemiologic Catchment Area Program. Historical context, major objectives, and study population characteristics. *Archives of General Psychiatry,* 41, pp. 934-941.

Report and minutes of evidence of the commissioners of inquiry into the state of lunatic asylums in Ireland 1858.

Report of the Commission on the Relief of the Sick and Destitute Poor, including the Insane Poor – 1927.

Reynolds J (1992) *Grangegorman Psychiatric Care in Dublin since 1815.* Dublin: Institute of Public Administration in association with the Eastern Health Board.

Robins J (1986) *Fools and Mad.* Dublin: The Institute of Public Administration.

Scull A (1979) *Museums of Madness.* London: Allan Lane.

Special Report from the Inspectors of Lunatics to the Chief Secretary. (1894) *Alleged Increasing Prevalence of Insanity in Ireland.* Dublin: HMSO.

Tagliavini A (1985) *Aspects of the history of psychiatry in Italy in the second half of the nineteenth century.* In: The anatomy of madness Vol.2 Institutions and Society Eds. Bynum,WF, Porter, R and Shepherd,M. Tavistock Publications, London and New York.

Tuke DH (1894) Increase of insanity in Ireland. *Journal of Mental Science,* 40, pp. 549-558.

Walsh D (1968) Hospitalised Psychiatric Morbidity in the Republic of Ireland. *British Journal of Psychiatry,* 114, pp. 11-14.

Walsh D (1971) *The 1963 Irish Psychiatric Hospital Census.* Dublin: Medico-Social Research Board.

Walsh D & Walsh B (1970) Mental illness in the Republic of Ireland – First admissions. *Journal of the Irish Medical Association,* 63, 400, pp. 365-370.

Walton JK (1983). Casting out and bringing back in Victorian England: pauper lunatics, 1840 – 70. In: *The Anatomy of Madness, Vol 2 Institutions and Society.* Eds. Bynum WF, Porter R and Shepherd M. London and New York, Tavistock Publications.

World Health Organisation (WHO) (1974) Glossary of Mental Disorders and Guide to their Classification for use in conjunction with the International Classification of Diseases, 8th Revision. Geneva: WHO.

World Health Organisation (WHO) (1978) Mental Disorders: Glossary and Guide to their Classification in Accordance with the Ninth Revision of the International Classification of Diseases. Geneva: WHO.

World Health Organization (WHO) (2001) *Atlas Country Profiles of Mental Health Resources* 2001. Geneva: WHO.

World Health Organisation (WHO) (1992) The ICD-10 Classification of Mental and Behavioural Disorders. Clinical Description and Diagnostic Guidelines. Geneva: WHO.

APPENDICES

Table 2.1a   Number of residents in district and auxiliary hospitals at 31 December 1914-1962.

Year	Male	Female	Total	Year	Male	Female	Total
1914	na	na	16,941	1939	10,018	9,024	19,042
1915	na	na	16,957	1940	10,057	9,077	19,134
1916	na	na	16,784	1941	9,809	8,937	18,746
1917	na	na	16,211	1942	9,477	8,654	18,131
1918	na	na	15,714	1943	9,176	8,555	17,731
1919	na	na	15,515	1944	9,090	8,516	17,606
1920	na	na	15,331	1945	9,136	8,572	17,708
1921	na	na	15,552	1946	9,143	8,648	17,791
1922	na	na	15,867	1947	9,022	8,613	17,635
1923	na	na	16,106	1948	9,178	8,816	17,994
1924	8,749	7,549	16,298	1949	9,491	8,986	18,477
1925	8,874	7,630	16,504	1950	9,580	9,097	18,677
1926	8,966	7,742	16,708	1951	9,644	9,153	18,797
1927	8,990	7,844	16,834	1952	9,817	9,250	19,067
1928	9,143	7,944	17,087	1953	10,033	9,439	19,472
1929	9,255	8,124	17,379	1954	10,189	9,545	19,734
1930	9,291	8,163	17,454	1955	10,309	9,501	19,810
1931	9,400	8,184	17,584	1956	10,457	9,606	20,063
1932	9,516	8,312	17,828	1957	10,512	9,296	19,808
1933	9,704	8,531	18,235	1958	na	na	na
1934	9,826	8,599	18,425	1959	10,574	9,016	19,590
1935	9,848	8,658	18,506	1960	10,494	8,948	19,442
1936	9,935	8,806	18,741	1961	10,279	8,798	19,077
1937	9,878	8,794	18,672	1962	10,095	8,548	18,643
1938	9,998	8,949	18,947				

na Not Available

Table 2.2a   Number of residents in private and charitable institutions 1932-1962.

Year	Male	Female	Total	Year	Male	Female	Total
1932	319	484	803	1948	390	488	878
1933	308	483	791	1949	288	509	797
1934	308	471	779	1950	381	510	891
1935	292	472	764	1951	370	511	881
1936	293	491	784	1952	389	486	875
1937	288	475	763	1953	408	546	954
1938	285	446	731	1954	367	558	925
1939	na	na	na	1955	392	536	928
1940	na	na	na	1956	409	571	980
1941	na	na	na	1957	428	544	972
1942	267	375	642	1958	na	na	na
1943	248	391	639	1959	426	593	1,019
1944	239	375	614	1960	447	617	1,064
1945	238	359	597	1961	425	597	1,022
1946	231	330	561	1962	411	602	1,013
1947	385	497	882				

Table 3.1a All and first admissions to Irish psychiatric hospitals, units and children's centres 1965–2002. Numbers with rates per 100,000 total population.

Year	All	First	Year	All	First
1965	15,440	6,210	1965	535.4	215.0
1966	16,526	6,676	1966	573.0	232.0
1967	17,607	6,927	1967	611.0	240.0
1968	18,953	7,284	1968	657.0	252.0
1969	19,697	7,652	1969	683.0	263.0
1970	20,342	7,696	1970	705.0	267.0
1971	21,351	8,058	1971	740.3	279.4
1972	22,964	8,598	1972	796.2	298.1
1973	24,036	9,018	1973	833.4	312.6
1974	24,964	8,914	1974	838.2	299.3
1975	25,892	8,873	1975	869.3	297.9
1976	26,434	8,939	1976	887.5	300.1
1977	26,385	8,788	1977	885.9	295.0
1978	27,662	8,678	1978	928.8	291.3
1979	27,358	8,631	1979	812.1	256.2
1980	27,098	8,459	1980	804.4	251.1
1981	28,685	8,480	1981	851.5	251.7
1982	28,778	8,702	1982	854.3	258.3
1983	28,397	8,415	1983	824.6	244.3
1984	28,830	8,749	1984	837.2	254.0
1985	29,082	8,441	1985	844.5	245.1
1986	29,392	8,251	1986	853.5	239.6
1987	27,856	7,934	1987	809.0	230.4
1988	28,432	8,074	1988	825.6	234.4
1989	27,250	7,530	1989	769.6	212.7
1990	27,765	7,577	1990	784.2	214.0
1991	27,913	7,949	1991	788.4	224.5
1992	27,148	7,443	1992	766.8	210.2
1993	27,005	7,311	1993	762.7	206.5
1994	26,687	7,132	1994	753.7	201.4
1995	26,440	7,246	1995	749.9	205.5
1996	26,985	7,191	1996	765.4	204.0
1997	26,069	7,049	1997	718.9	194.4
1998	25,295	7,137	1998	697.6	196.8
1999	25,118	7,147	1999	692.7	197.1
2000	24,343	7,338	2000	671.3	202.4
2001	24,507	7,348	2001	675.9	202.6
2002	23,736	7,111	2002	605.9	181.5

Table 3.2a All and first admissions by gender 1965–2002. Rates per 100,000 total population.

	All Admissions			First Admissions		
	Male	Female	Total	Male	Female	Total
1965	551.2	519.4	535.4	226.2	204.3	215.3
1966	584.7	561.3	573.0	242.9	219.9	231.5
1967	630.3	590.5	610.5	257.9	222.2	240.2
1968	702.1	610.0	657.2	273.4	230.6	252.6
1969	708.7	649.8	683.0	277.4	249.3	265.3
1970	736.6	670.0	705.3	283.4	248.5	266.9
1971	777.2	755.1	740.3	296.6	262.0	279.4
1972	836.9	703.0	796.2	317.9	278.1	298.1
1973	897.3	768.8	833.4	336.2	288.8	312.6
1974	897.8	778.0	838.2	324.5	273.8	299.3
1975	930.4	807.7	869.3	321.9	273.6	297.9
1976	938.0	836.6	887.5	320.7	279.3	300.1
1977	951.5	819.7	885.9	324.1	265.7	295.0
1978	1,010.1	846.6	928.8	324.5	257.9	291.3
1979	895.3	728.2	812.2	291.4	220.6	256.2
1980	875.9	732.2	804.5	280.3	221.6	251.1
1981	931.0	771.3	851.6	284.1	219.0	251.7
1982	925.5	782.4	854.3	285.4	230.9	258.3
1983	903.1	745.5	824.6	273.4	215.0	244.3
1984	908.6	765.2	837.2	280.4	227.4	254.0
1985	918.0	770.4	844.5	279.2	210.7	245.1
1986	926.4	780.0	853.5	270.2	208.2	239.6
1987	870.3	747.0	809.0	259.3	201.2	230.4
1988	894.2	756.5	825.6	263.2	205.4	234.4
1989	831.6	707.8	769.6	241.6	183.7	212.7
1990	850.7	717.7	784.2	242.6	185.4	214.0
1991	865.2	711.6	788.4	258.1	190.9	224.5
1992	830.1	703.4	766.8	235.9	184.5	210.2
1993	823.1	702.3	762.7	228.1	184.9	206.5
1994	827.5	680.0	753.7	230.0	172.8	201.4
1995	819.8	680.8	749.9	230.8	180.5	205.5
1996	825.2	706.1	765.4	223.7	184.4	204.0
1997	785.2	653.6	718.9	222.7	166.4	194.4
1998	762.5	633.6	697.6	225.0	169.0	196.8
1999	765.8	620.6	692.7	225.9	168.7	197.1
2000	721.9	621.5	671.3	228.7	176.4	202.4
2001	720.2	632.1	675.9	227.6	178.0	202.6
2002	629.2	583.0	605.9	201.3	162.0	181.5

Table 3.3a All admissions by age 1965–2002. Rates per 100,000 total population.

	< 15	15–19	20–24	25–34	35–44	45–54	55–64	65–69	70–79	80 & over	65–74	75 & over
1965	19.0	209.4	513.3	913.7	952.7	905.4	940.9	902.6	786.1	463.5		
1966	24.3	250.2	589.9	634.9	1,078.6	958.4	946.5	892.1	782.2	538.6		
1967	21.9	270.3	630.4	1,021.1	1,109.5	1,024.2	1,039.9	952.5	896.7	570.9		
1968	16.3	294.6	715.1	1,071.2	1,193.2	1,129.5	1,107.8	1,029.5	941.8	613.8		
1969	14.3	311.2	770.7	1,121.2	1,217.4	1,145.5	1,207.1	1,108.3	888.8	689.0		
1970	15.4	304.2	810.6	1,173.9	1,250.5	1,185.6	1,221.5	1,132.0	964.0	594.1		
1971	23.5	309.9	813.3	1,264.7	1,355.3	1,288.4	1,226.6				1,152.5	700.1
1972	19.4	303.4	936.3	1,372.8	1,412.5	1,384.1	1,346.6				1,235.7	805.5
1973	16.9	281.4	1,013.5	1,507.3	1,511.4	1,445.0	1,373.1				1,246.4	805.5
1974	13.1	293.9	930.5	1,444.7	1,652.1	1,526.6	1,393.1				1,197.7	803.6
1975	15.8	300.3	882.6	1,592.0	1,763.5	1,517.8	1,425.6				1,236.5	825.4
1976	10.4	272.2	947.7	1,625.6	1,767.8	1,568.5	1,421.5				1,294.4	938.0
1977	9.4	274.1	832.5	1,667.9	1,749.2	1,546.0	1,464.8				1,338.0	918.6
1978	7.3	250.6	859.4	1,748.1	1,843.3	1,652.5	1,539.9				1,374.6	1,022.8
1979	9.6	207.6	681.2	1,165.2	1,627.7	1,691.3	1,515.0				1,346.5	960.5
1980	14.5	210.7	648.5	1,146.3	1,659.9	1,618.0	1,451.2				1,376.6	1,024.7
1981	12.9	222.1	701.9	1,256.4	1,734.8	1,708.4	1,586.3				1,396.0	988.3
1982	11.2	233.4	714.6	1,319.1	1,735.4	1,661.8	1,547.6				1,398.6	987.5
1983	9.7	200.9	677.2	1,234.2	1,634.9	1,616.7	1,568.1				1,372.6	1,006.8
1984	8.7	192.9	681.9	1,220.4	1,735.5	1,679.4	1,542.8				1,421.1	953.7
1985	10.7	204.6	646.8	1,188.4	1,768.9	1,657.8	1,588.5				1,444.3	1,106.1
1986	13.3	202.1	679.3	1,236.7	1,759.5	1,675.7	1,533.8				1,439.6	1,196.3
1987	12.9	204.6	623.2	1,125.8	1,739.1	1,599.1	1,453.5				1,385.7	1,051.5
1988	14.2	204.9	628.6	1,151.9	1,804.5	1,629.6	1,440.7				1,371.7	1,175.9
1989	12.0	216.2	559.7	1,057.4	1,506.1	1,556.7	1,346.2				1,215.8	1,033.6
1990	11.1	228.9	576.1	1,111.9	1,481.9	1,563.8	1,379.2				1,235.4	1,101.8
1991	12.9	224.7	588.6	1,115.3	1,521.3	1,595.1	1,361.1				1,230.4	1,013.5
1992	15.2	235.0	608.9	1,077.8	1,486.6	1,548.3	1,258.0				1,208.8	1,003.1
1993	12.7	255.5	641.0	1,090.9	1,450.6	1,556.3	1,228.2				1,121.0	1,026.7
1994	20.3	247.1	618.7	1,072.2	1,434.4	1,526.6	1,220.8				1,159.3	978.0
1995	35.0	184.0	565.7	815.3	1,100.5	1,282.6	1,164.0				1,178.3	996.6
1996	36.9	306.6	661.0	966.6	1,201.7	1,210.1	1,159.2				1,026.9	862.9
1997	18.0	296.5	702.9	929.9	1,177.9	1,225.8	1,140.7				945.5	838.2
1998	14.0	317.4	682.5	955.8	1,126.5	1,195.0	1,075.2				918.7	803.3
1999	12.0	309.9	720.3	976.0	1,105.4	1,188.9	1,056.4				913.3	755.2
2000	9.7	302.5	713.5	933.7	1,099.1	1,129.2	1,067.3				851.9	681.3
2001	7.5	295.0	668.8	915.0	1,132.0	1,160.5	1,091.7				850.2	709.9
2002	8.1	294.5	587.8	758.1	932.9	982.6	908.3				800.1	607.7

Table 3.4a All admissions by marital status 1965–2002. Numbers with rates per 100,000 total population.

Year	Single	Married	Widowed	Divorced	Unspecified	Single	Married	Widowed	Divorced	Unspecified
	Numbers					Rates				
1965	8,553	5,486	1,395	-	6	-	-	-	-	-
1966	9,255	5,855	1,415	-	1	-	-	-	-	-
1967	9,419	6,681	1,499	-	8	-	-	-	-	-
1968	10,051	7,275	1,563	-	64	-	-	-	-	-
1969	10,441	7,499	1,619	-	138	-	-	-	-	-
1970	10,504	7,907	1,798	-	133	-	-	-	-	-
1971	10,991	8,477	1,762	-	121	627.5	877.4	1,057.9	-	-
1972	11,749	9,159	1,937	-	119	670.8	948.0	1,162.9	-	-
1973	12,030	9,884	1,970	-	152	686.8	1,023.1	1,182.8	-	-
1974	12,417	10,441	1,937	-	169	701.0	1,005.8	1,146.7	-	-
1975	12,633	10,965	2,059	-	235	713.1	1,056.3	1,218.9	-	-
1976	12,759	11,197	2,134	-	344	720.3	1,078.7	1,263.4	-	-
1977	12,606	11,280	2,077	-	422	711.6	1,086.7	1,229.6	-	-
1978	13,048	11,993	2,069	-	552	736.6	1,155.3	1,224.9	-	-
1979	12,956	11,688	2,157	-	557	666.7	937.5	1,208.5	-	-
1980	12,837	11,377	2,214	-	670	660.6	912.6	1,240.4	-	-
1981	13,862	11,677	2,271	-	875	713.4	936.7	1,272.4	-	-
1982	13,746	11,701	2,298	-	1,033	707.4	938.6	1,287.5	-	-
1983	13,665	11,429	2,283	-	1,020	691.7	887.3	1,270.9	-	-
1984	13,770	11,377	2,348	-	1,335	696.9	883.2	1,307.1	-	-
1985	14,235	11,229	2,372	-	1,246	720.5	871.8	1,320.5	-	-
1986	14,417	11,087	2,478	-	1,410	729.7	860.7	1,379.5	-	-
1987	13,584	10,559	2,155	-	1,558	687.6	819.7	1,199.7	-	-
1988	13,937	10,569	2,257	-	1,669	705.4	820.5	1,256.5	-	-
1989	13,583	9,719	2,062	-	1,886	674.8	745.3	1,106.7	-	-
1990	14,022	9,689	2,113	-	1,941	696.6	743.0	1,134.1	-	-
1991	14,137	9,382	2,189	-	2,205	702.3	719.4	1,174.8	-	-
1992	14,040	8,957	2,119	-	2,032	697.5	686.8	1,137.3	-	-
1993	14,016	8,620	1,933	-	2,436	696.3	661.0	1,037.5	-	-
1994	13,933	8,428	1,912	-	2,414	692.2	646.3	1,026.2	-	-
1995	14,162	7,948	1,905	-	2,425	725.0	597.9	1,014.9	-	-
1996	14,256	7,909	1,829	-	2,991	729.8	594.9	974.4	-	-
1997	13,723	7,719	1,790	-	2,837	687.1	569.0	970.7	-	-
1998	13,421	7,290	1,685	-	2,899	672.0	537.4	913.8	-	-
1999	13,773	6,940	1,503	-	2,902	689.6	511.6	815.1	-	-
2000	13,269	6,990	1,393	86	2,605	664.4	515.3	755.4	878.7	-
2001	13,179	7,031	1,290	149	2,858	659.8	518.3	699.6	1,522.4	-
2002	12,809	6,805	1,224	220	2,678	598.0	467.9	655.0	627.5	-

Table 3.5a All admissions by socio-economic group 1965–2002. Rates per 100,000 total population.

	F	OA	HP	LP	EM	SE	INM	ONM	SM	SS	US
1971	460.2	915.2	836.6	908.4	477.1	427.6	546.5	880.5	422.5	628.4	832.7
1972	571.5	1,121.0	1,012.7	1,092.5	576.3	567.7	811.4	1,194.9	605.7	730.1	1,231.9
1973	595.8	1,077.3	1,040.2	1,097.9	675.5	700.7	843.4	1,263.9	660.6	556.3	1,636.8
1974	712.5	1,287.0	947.7	951.2	535.4	612.9	913.9	1,311.7	666.8	542.5	1,608.9
1975	722.7	1,153.6	1,024.9	987.3	581.6	518.9	941.1	1,292.9	728.6	631.2	1,796.5
1976	767.3	1,167.6	979.0	1,019.9	505.1	510.5	992.8	1,280.0	778.4	706.6	1,707.0
1977	732.4	1,085.7	885.0	972.9	487.9	596.1	1,042.3	1,274.8	651.6	982.5	1,846.8
1978	767.5	1,275.3	862.7	1,058.8	505.8	537.4	1,094.9	1,303.1	705.6	1,046.4	1,766.2
1979	672.9	1,131.1	720.2	948.9	354.1	503.3	958.2	1,113.1	630.0	899.7	1,622.3
1980	641.3	975.1	796.4	930.5	345.1	709.7	950.3	1,057.7	652.8	853.4	1,621.6
1981	649.8	936.4	811.2	877.0	356.2	772.1	1,011.3	1,186.6	685.7	954.2	1,703.8
1982	634.1	841.2	747.9	917.7	369.0	715.7	1,075.7	1,157.4	734.8	857.5	1,702.1
1983	925.9	1,119.2	626.8	672.9	256.5	566.7	975.5	1,055.2	614.1	770.6	2,226.4
1984	894.6	1,057.7	628.4	734.9	375.1	672.3	918.6	1,109.2	567.2	899.9	2,313.8
1985	901.9	1,113.3	612.2	749.4	440.8	538.6	922.0	1,093.0	543.5	989.2	2,360.9
1986	889.3	1,002.1	604.5	803.8	428.9	648.2	924.1	1,084.2	481.0	1,061.1	2,368.6
1987	778.4	826.5	559.7	744.7	349.5	522.6	877.1	1,045.0	447.1	856.0	2,216.5
1988	714.5	841.4	494.1	695.5	245.4	629.5	908.9	990.7	522.8	921.9	2,240.5
1989	681.0	750.1	416.5	570.8	197.1	455.9	696.6	793.9	441.8	790.4	2,089.0
1990	706.1	725.8	490.2	576.3	237.5	458.4	672.4	843.7	453.7	906.0	2,103.0
1991	668.1	796.8	568.9	575.3	272.8	496.5	638.8	789.2	453.0	887.8	1,927.3
1992	627.8	602.4	646.8	600.0	228.7	542.3	568.7	816.7	380.3	901.7	1,659.1
1993	540.6	611.2	594.1	622.1	200.9	486.4	563.4	749.7	383.8	793.8	1,420.4
1994	504.4	638.4	607.9	571.3	201.3	596.9	517.1	641.2	362.6	777.0	1,320.6
1995	531.7	546.6	534.7	462.6	197.5	564.2	413.5	683.0	393.7	962.8	1,112.5
1996	489.1	608.8	521.5	471.2	233.1	537.2	423.7	643.2	344.1	1,037.4	976.2

	F	AW	HP	LP	EM	OAW	NM	MS	SS	US
1997	547.7	614.7	354.5	366.1	114.4	250.0	767.7	371.0	472.8	817.9
1998	467.8	512.5	391.2	394.3	155.6	366.7	774.5	352.9	467.9	894.0
1999	443.5	485.0	347.0	375.0	117.6	369.1	568.6	308.4	366.0	828.0
2000	399.9	313.3	322.8	501.1	168.2	42.3	442.2	388.2	288.1	883.2
2001	321.6	309.3	334.6	465.6	136.7	118.6	476.6	426.7	398.1	894.4
2002	391.6	553.9	363.8	408.7	115.9	111.2	479.6	650.1	478.4	1,236.6

F=Farmers OA=Other Agricultural Workers HP=Higher Professional LP=Lower Professional EM=Employers & Managers SE=Salaried Employees INM=Intermediate Non-Manual ONM=Other Non-Manual SM=Skilled Manual SS=Semi-Skilled US=Unskilled AW=Agricultural Workers OAW=Own Account Workers NM=Non-manual MS=Non-manual Skilled.

Table 3.6a All admissions by diagnosis 1965–2002. Rates per 100,000 total population.

	Organic psychoses	Schizophrenia	Affective disorders	Neuroses	Personality disorders	Alcoholic disorders	Drug dependence	Mental handicap	Unspecified
1965	53.7	162.4	-	106.9	7.2	56.8	2.9	19.5	2.1
1966	56.2	172.2	-	120.7	7.6	60.9	2.2	19.3	0.9
1967	59.9	178.1	-	131.2	9.6	69.8	2.4	19.9	0.6
1968	60.7	180.9	-	143.3	9.1	87.6	3.4	21.6	15.7
1969	61.5	185.7	-	149.9	11.4	100.1	4.1	22.4	5.7
1970	61.3	189.4	-	162.0	11.6	106.6	5.0	23.2	7.4
1971	47.9	227.9	203.3	99.2	26.5	128.9	4.8	27.1	11.2
1972	54.9	242.1	237.7	99.4	32.1	143.6	5.3	25.6	9.6
1973	50.5	255.9	234.2	96.8	34.8	168.0	7.7	24.8	12.8
1974	48.4	252.8	255.2	96.5	34.7	179.8	6.5	22.8	13.0
1975	46.8	253.8	245.8	103.7	35.6	201.5	6.1	24.1	12.5
1976	46.3	255.8	251.3	109.2	41.0	204.8	5.3	24.0	14.8
1977	41.7	246.5	250.7	101.8	35.0	227.1	6.1	22.5	12.6
1978	42.2	254.6	261.2	122.3	38.3	244.8	4.4	19.8	14.0
1979	36.9	223.7	235.3	102.6	30.8	212.5	3.8	17.7	13.0
1980	42.6	226.6	167.7	99.0	29.6	208.4	3.2	14.8	12.3
1981	39.9	198.7	286.7	48.5	35.1	218.0	7.2	12.7	4.4
1982	36.3	199.2	297.2	49.1	37.1	213.4	6.5	12.0	3.4
1983	37.2	185.5	292.3	45.5	34.7	206.1	7.2	11.5	4.2
1984	31.9	186.2	302.1	47.1	38.5	208.8	5.6	13.1	3.6
1985	36.1	181.0	309.8	46.9	37.6	211.1	5.8	11.7	4.2
1986	35.4	181.1	311.8	37.6	35.0	207.1	7.3	14.4	23.6
1987	29.2	168.5	301.2	39.1	31.7	188.5	6.6	11.9	32.0
1988	26.2	185.5	306.8	36.3	30.8	188.1	7.1	12.9	31.7
1989	24.0	174.7	271.6	39.1	37.8	186.6	5.5	13.1	17.4
1990	24.3	180.0	293.0	42.4	40.5	180.1	7.6	12.4	3.9
1991	21.9	176.2	288.6	47.3	40.3	186.2	7.8	12.7	7.3
1992	22.3	172.7	285.2	43.6	41.1	171.7	9.3	10.8	10.0
1993	20.6	168.4	291.6	44.4	42.8	161.5	10.8	12.8	9.8
1994	22.3	164.8	280.1	47.1	41.7	156.8	14.5	13.6	12.8
1995	23.1	163.6	283.5	44.8	39.6	149.2	15.3	19.0	11.7
1996	24.3	166.4	277.9	50.3	42.7	154.0	16.0	19.2	14.3
1997	26.5	151.9	264.5	43.5	39.2	144.8	15.9	12.2	20.4
1998	23.9	136.6	273.7	46.5	37.6	139.4	19.0	11.3	9.4
1999	19.8	145.1	274.0	41.5	37.1	134.0	19.6	9.5	12.0
2000	20.0	141.5	278.9	39.1	32.6	124.6	18.3	7.6	8.8
2001	18.8	142.2	292.7	36.3	28.2	120.4	20.5	8.1	8.6
2002	13.5	120.5	275.9	31.3	25.6	101.0	17.2	6.7	14.3

Table 3.7a All admissions by gender for schizophrenia, affective disorders and alcoholic disorders 1965–2002. Rates per 100,000 population.

	Schizophrenia		Affective disorders		Alcoholic disorders	
	Male	Female	Male	Female	Male	Female
1965	186.1	138.6	–	–	95.1	18.1
1966	196.3	147.9	–	–	100.8	20.7
1967	207.7	148.3	–	–	114.0	25.2
1968	213.2	147.9	–	–	149.8	24.5
1969	209.3	159.7	–	–	170.0	28.6
1970	215.2	162.0	–	–	180.1	31.8
1971	241.5	214.2	149.6	257.6	214.3	43.3
1972	245.9	238.3	177.3	298.6	242.9	42.7
1973	271.4	240.4	175.1	293.9	278.5	56.4
1974	266.0	239.5	191.9	319.0	297.5	61.0
1975	273.5	233.9	177.2	315.1	326.7	75.2
1976	262.9	248.7	180.3	323.0	330.8	77.7
1977	252.3	240.7	182.8	319.1	368.7	84.3
1978	267.0	242.2	192.5	330.4	398.9	89.3
1979	241.2	206.0	182.3	288.8	342.7	80.8
1980	249.3	203.6	119.6	216.4	333.8	81.6
1981	234.5	162.6	206.3	367.9	353.3	81.2
1982	228.1	169.9	218.0	377.2	344.8	80.5
1983	217.9	152.9	214.1	371.2	337.3	73.8
1984	215.5	156.6	221.4	383.5	338.3	78.2
1985	208.4	153.4	232.5	387.7	342.0	79.1
1986	211.6	150.4	237.0	387.3	330.9	82.1
1987	193.8	143.0	235.1	368.0	298.7	77.3
1988	215.9	154.7	244.9	369.2	297.6	77.6
1989	195.7	153.6	215.3	327.8	290.1	83.2
1990	206.9	153.1	234.7	351.3	282.2	78.1
1991	205.7	146.8	230.6	346.6	288.9	83.6
1992	195.3	150.1	228.9	341.4	270.1	73.5
1993	196.3	140.6	239.6	343.6	248.9	74.1
1994	193.5	136.2	231.0	329.1	243.7	70.0
1995	198.5	129.0	237.0	329.5	222.3	77.0
1996	194.8	138.2	231.7	323.6	232.2	77.0
1997	183.1	121.1	221.6	306.8	216.7	73.9
1998	168.5	105.2	236.8	310.1	208.1	71.7
1999	179.7	111.0	242.9	304.8	201.1	67.8
2000	173.6	109.9	240.5	316.8	182.2	67.7
2001	174.6	110.2	251.1	333.7	170.1	71.4
2002	146.2	95.1	236.3	315.0	138.1	64.3

Table 3.8a All non-voluntary admissions 1971-2002. Percentages with rates per 100,000 population.

	Percentage			Rate		
	Male	Female	Total	Male	Female	Total
1971	18.9	16.0	17.6	147.1	112.8	130.0
1972	17.8	15.2	16.6	148.7	114.8	131.9
1973	18.6	14.0	16.5	166.6	108.0	137.4
1974	17.4	14.6	16.1	161.1	117.5	139.4
1975	17.0	14.2	15.7	157.7	114.4	136.2
1976	17.1	13.1	15.3	160.8	110.0	135.5
1977	16.7	12.9	15.0	159.1	105.8	132.6
1978	15.8	12.0	14.1	159.3	101.7	130.6
1979	15.2	11.7	13.6	153.7	96.5	125.2
1980	14.2	11.5	13.0	141.1	94.8	118.1
1981	13.6	10.5	12.2	143.5	91.1	117.4
1982	-	-	-	-	-	-
1983	13.8	10.9	12.5	124.8	81.2	103.1
1984	13.2	11.2	12.3	120.3	86.1	103.2
1985	13.4	11.1	12.3	122.8	85.2	104.1
1986	13.2	10.4	11.9	122.2	80.7	101.6
1987	12.6	9.7	11.3	108.7	72.1	90.5
1988	-	-	-	-	-	-
1989	13.9	12.0	13.0	115.8	85.0	100.4
1990	13.1	9.5	11.5	111.5	68.2	89.8
1991	13.0	10.2	11.7	112.3	72.9	92.6
1992	11.9	9.6	10.9	98.9	67.5	83.2
1993	12.5	9.3	11.0	102.9	65.2	84.0
1994	11.7	10.0	11.0	97.2	68.0	82.6
1995	12.1	9.4	10.9	98.9	64.2	81.5
1996	11.7	10.4	11.1	96.9	73.2	85.0
1997	12.3	9.3	10.9	96.5	61.0	78.6
1998	11.2	8.8	10.1	85.6	55.8	70.6
1999	12.2	9.3	10.9	93.2	57.8	75.3
2000	11.9	9.4	10.7	85.8	58.6	72.1
2001	11.9	9.7	10.9	85.9	61.4	73.6
2002	12.8	10.0	11.4	80.5	58.3	69.4

Table 3.9a All admissions by health board areas 1972–2002. Rates per 100,000 total population.

	EHB/EHRA	MHB	MWHB	NEHB	NWHB	SEHB	SHB	WHB
1972	827.8	708.7	846.6	684.2	773.1	912.5	752.7	703.4
1973	862.1	651.5	884.8	705.8	775.8	925.6	816.5	793.7
1974	839.7	642.2	968.1	753.8	839.6	942.7	778.2	831.6
1975	865.6	667.9	1,042.2	763.6	917.7	1,015.2	793.9	807.3
1976	852.9	775.8	1,045.2	771.7	830.7	1,021.8	858.5	829.0
1977	865.3	766.8	1,079.3	824.7	996.9	1,026.7	818.6	738.4
1978	918.5	806.0	1,081.5	885.3	1,039.6	1,059.6	871.0	766.0
1979	759.1	749.1	954.1	777.3	1,050.9	993.2	626.7	834.1
1980	692.7	753.7	1,010.2	753.8	1,068.0	992.6	701.4	825.4
1981	735.2	803.7	1,128.9	709.3	1,076.8	991.8	788.0	922.7
1982	732.3	859.8	1,163.2	694.4	967.2	1,015.0	797.9	934.9
1983	718.3	838.0	1,102.4	648.4	915.4	977.9	774.7	918.7
1984	752.4	782.6	1,071.9	712.8	933.2	968.0	777.1	918.1
1985	761.5	816.2	1,120.9	655.0	869.8	1,010.2	795.4	906.1
1986	807.5	762.3	1,005.8	703.1	857.8	1,039.8	789.5	920.8
1987	803.3	726.7	997.3	624.6	931.9	949.8	676.8	864.8
1988	849.0	786.0	994.7	666.8	799.2	920.5	671.3	872.7
1989	774.5	823.6	860.7	610.2	758.7	892.8	642.0	818.8
1990	796.3	719.3	847.1	651.9	808.5	902.4	682.1	817.3
1991	801.4	695.2	766.2	637.3	825.4	906.0	723.4	856.7
1992	801.3	665.4	728.2	565.5	796.3	844.2	710.4	872.2
1993	794.7	654.8	722.2	532.1	903.4	797.7	711.3	881.1
1994	811.9	610.1	726.3	534.4	924.6	766.0	685.6	809.0
1995	789.8	698.1	720.6	514.4	880.5	783.7	695.3	799.8
1996	823.6	700.5	704.2	511.7	914.1	786.0	675.8	866.5
1997	744.2	732.2	671.1	473.0	855.5	754.8	668.8	799.5
1998	732.6	753.1	657.6	457.9	775.4	736.9	640.5	748.1
1999	726.2	784.8	631.7	435.4	757.3	786.4	587.8	781.6
2000	643.7	811.5	646.9	409.3	718.9	792.6	665.9	753.5
2001	640.0	863.6	636.1	388.4	822.3	776.0	640.8	790.7
2002	588.8	725.9	558.0	352.8	649.9	730.6	591.5	704.4

Table 3.10a All admissions by hospital type 1965–2002. Percentages.

	Local authority hospitals/ Health board hospitals	General hospital units	Private hospitals	Children's centres
1965	75.9	0.0	24.1	0.0
1966	77.2	0.0	22.8	0.0
1967	77.7	0.3	22.0	0.0
1968	77.2	0.7	22.1	0.0
1969	74.8	3.7	21.5	0.0
1970	74.3	4.6	21.1	0.0
1971	71.5	8.4	20.0	0.0
1972	71.7	9.0	19.4	0.0
1973	71.1	9.9	19.1	0.0
1974	70.5	11.0	18.5	0.0
1975	71.0	10.9	18.0	0.2
1976	71.4	11.7	16.8	0.1
1977	69.0	13.6	17.4	0.0
1978	69.7	13.6	16.7	0.0
1979	69.2	12.9	17.7	0.2
1980	67.2	15.4	17.1	0.3
1981	67.1	16.8	15.8	0.3
1982	67.8	16.4	15.4	0.3
1983	68.5	16.0	15.2	0.3
1984	68.8	15.9	15.1	0.2
1985	68.7	16.2	14.7	0.3
1986	68.2	16.1	15.3	0.4
1987	66.6	16.7	16.4	0.3
1988	65.2	17.8	16.5	0.4
1989	68.2	16.8	14.5	0.5
1990	62.4	20.5	16.5	0.5
1991	60.7	23.6	15.3	0.5
1992	55.4	29.3	14.5	0.8
1993	55.0	29.1	15.1	0.9
1994	53.6	29.6	15.7	1.1
1995	53.9	28.9	16.1	1.2
1996	53.4	30.0	15.4	1.2
1997	51.8	32.2	15.7	0.3
1998	52.5	31.4	15.9	0.2
1999	48.7	36.2	14.8	0.2
2000	46.8	39.1	13.9	0.3
2001	44.0	42.2	13.5	0.2
2002	41.0	41.1	17.6	0.2

Table 3.11a First admissions by age 1965–2002. Rates per 100,000 total population.

	<15	15–19	20–24	25–34	35–44	45–54	55–64	65–69	70–79	80 & over
1965	10.4	132.3	252.0	367.0	344.1	320.7	335.9	349.3	366.9	341.8
1966	12.7	153.5	304.9	400.1	396.7	331.2	324.8	329.2	372.1	411.6
1967	12.0	155.4	298.5	390.6	397.9	357.5	363.6	346.7	424.5	404.4
1968	9.8	182.4	362.7	410.6	399.8	375.6	374.7	340.6	439.5	411.6
1969	9.1	185.5	371.9	430.5	418.4	389.2	414.9	383.5	421.8	499.3
1970	9.6	189.3	379.9	467.7	424.7	382.8	394.6	396.6	411.4	413.4
	<15	15–19	20–24	25–34	35–44	45–54	55–64	65–74	75 & over	80 & over
1971	15.3	187.0	389.1	507.8	465.2	422.6	379.1	409.5	394.3	–
1972	13.3	180.0	441.4	554.4	475.3	425.9	450.3	435.0	438.9	–
1973	9.5	171.9	493.2	619.3	529.5	459.1	416.0	449.7	412.0	–
1974	9.4	179.6	426.4	534.2	543.9	463.0	417.7	405.2	430.7	–
1975	9.7	180.7	398.6	587.9	532.7	449.5	407.3	400.9	393.0	–
1976	5.6	161.7	424.6	569.0	539.6	447.6	402.5	427.0	480.3	–
1977	5.3	159.8	389.7	588.5	523.0	424.8	418.1	421.3	445.9	–
1978	5.0	141.9	385.5	587.0	531.7	409.4	382.8	410.4	532.4	–
1979	7.4	128.8	310.9	401.1	460.4	442.9	370.1	381.2	467.8	–
1980	9.8	124.4	287.3	389.6	479.0	422.1	334.2	391.2	480.2	–
1981	7.5	128.5	307.9	410.8	479.1	399.1	360.9	358.0	440.0	–
1982	7.7	143.9	319.5	437.1	490.9	400.1	348.5	376.1	416.8	–
1983	5.9	119.7	308.9	403.0	450.2	372.1	349.2	372.0	416.2	–
1984	5.7	123.1	311.8	410.8	494.4	423.5	332.6	385.9	401.8	–
1985	7.9	127.1	285.7	385.7	480.8	377.4	333.3	380.0	438.9	–
1986	8.2	122.2	305.2	392.8	441.6	371.7	301.5	347.1	485.9	–
1987	8.1	129.5	268.7	353.2	476.6	364.4	295.2	341.1	393.4	–
1988	6.8	128.6	282.1	365.0	485.2	362.4	291.1	342.0	429.8	–
1989	7.0	125.3	237.1	312.9	395.0	343.1	284.6	284.8	351.0	–
1990	6.1	129.3	252.4	332.8	370.4	349.9	288.5	275.3	348.3	–
1991	8.2	130.8	276.5	335.4	396.2	372.8	287.4	294.4	374.0	–
1992	7.0	131.7	258.4	323.9	374.6	343.4	247.0	282.8	352.4	–
1993	7.2	130.2	277.2	317.5	359.2	347.3	244.9	238.3	348.3	–
1994	6.7	130.8	261.2	316.9	336.4	330.8	244.5	256.1	347.6	–
1995	10.4	119.1	314.7	315.1	315.2	300.1	242.5	254.5	327.3	–
1996	10.5	122.7	301.2	297.1	313.2	313.4	222.7	214.9	318.1	–
1997	11.2	162.4	288.4	287.3	280.6	260.9	213.5	210.6	273.9	–
1998	9.1	172.9	290.4	309.2	271.7	282.5	214.6	204.7	269.3	–
1999	9.2	173.3	309.9	310.0	281.8	252.4	225.5	220.6	252.1	–
2000	7.9	172.5	299.0	325.0	293.9	272.3	243.0	211.0	244.1	–
2001	5.8	171.4	300.0	303.5	309.4	271.3	262.2	220.6	229.2	–
2002	6.9	171.2	256.4	248.8	258.7	238.9	202.8	202.8	218.0	–

Table 3.12a First admissions by marital status 1965–2002. Numbers with rates per 100,000 total population.

| | Number | | | | | Rate | | | |
	Single	Married	Widowed	Divorced	Unspecified	Single	Married	Widowed	Divorced
1965	3,310	2,317	583	-	-	-	-	-	-
1966	3,553	2,514	608	-	1	-	-	-	-
1967	3,472	2,818	632	-	5	-	-	-	-
1968	3,646	2,963	650	-	25	-	-	-	-
1969	3,804	3,107	695	-	46	-	-	-	-
1970	3,683	3,221	739	-	53	-	-	-	-
1971	3,923	3,399	676	-	60	223.9	351.8	405.8	-
1972	4,165	3,642	733	-	58	237.8	376.9	440.1	-
1973	4,303	3,899	747	-	69	245.6	403.6	448.5	-
1974	4,218	3,927	693	-	76	238.1	378.3	410.2	-
1975	4,119	3,967	705	-	82	232.5	382.1	417.3	-
1976	4,039	4,051	732	-	117	228.0	390.2	433.3	-
1977	3,923	3,983	737	-	145	221.4	383.7	436.3	-
1978	3,772	3,958	715	-	233	212.9	381.3	423.3	-
1979	3,901	3,846	684	-	200	200.7	308.5	383.2	-
1980	3,744	3,730	731	-	254	192.7	299.2	409.6	-
1981	3,802	3,690	673	-	315	195.7	296.0	377.1	-
1982	3,877	3,771	710	-	344	199.5	302.5	397.8	-
1983	3,791	3,564	713	-	347	191.9	276.7	396.9	-
1984	3,880	3,710	711	-	448	196.3	288.0	395.8	-
1985	3,803	3,565	694	-	379	192.5	276.8	386.4	-
1986	3,813	3,363	668	-	407	193.0	261.1	371.8	-
1987	3,587	3,295	574	-	478	181.6	255.8	319.6	-
1988	3,634	3,337	629	-	474	183.9	259.1	350.2	-
1989	3,480	2,968	537	-	545	172.9	227.6	288.2	-
1990	3,601	2,886	551	-	539	178.9	221.3	295.7	-
1991	3,804	2,930	580	-	635	189.0	224.7	311.3	-
1992	3,672	2,695	570	-	506	182.4	206.7	305.9	-
1993	3,609	2,574	485	-	643	179.3	197.4	260.3	-
1994	3,565	2,453	465	-	649	177.1	188.1	249.6	-
1995	3,753	2,378	486	-	629	192.1	178.9	258.9	-
1996	3,554	2,287	475	-	875	181.9	172.0	253.1	-
1997	3,660	2,221	433	-	735	183.2	163.7	234.8	-
1998	3,721	2,199	443	-	774	186.3	162.1	240.2	-
1999	3,851	2,105	396	-	795	192.8	155.2	214.8	-
2000	3,959	2,202	400	32	745	198.2	162.3	216.9	327.0
2001	3,955	2,125	366	50	852	198.0	156.6	198.5	510.9
2002	3,766	2,182	368	78	717	175.8	150.0	196.9	222.5

Table 3.13a First admissions by socio-economic group 1971–2002. Rates per 100,000 total population.

	F	OA	HP	LP	EM	SE	INM	ONM	SM	SS	US	UNS
1971	160.6	268.3	387.1	423.3	206.4	192.2	225.4	288.3	173.0	229.5	264.8	1,452.8
1972	197.3	331.0	459.5	462.3	256.4	291.0	331.5	409.0	247.4	267.5	419.6	298.1
1973	206.9	305.7	428.3	478.5	338.6	318.0	332.1	450.0	275.2	211.2	567.4	166.3
1974	242.3	359.0	405.0	404.1	240.0	268.7	345.5	424.7	259.2	190.6	529.2	59.6
1975	229.0	284.8	464.3	408.6	240.7	194.8	345.8	396.3	270.6	214.2	583.0	46.9
1976	257.8	286.4	420.7	423.1	212.3	218.3	349.7	387.7	290.5	222.3	501.3	68.1
1977	223.4	287.2	369.2	384.2	205.7	260.3	370.9	388.7	240.1	324.8	541.6	75.5
1978	213.5	328.5	333.4	397.8	208.3	186.4	367.5	369.6	251.8	296.5	500.1	125.3
1979	182.4	285.0	262.1	365.3	142.8	185.6	339.4	316.8	220.2	279.0	462.1	102.1
1980	170.2	252.5	326.4	342.1	141.1	261.3	327.9	290.3	229.1	238.3	448.7	131.7
1981	155.9	207.0	279.9	287.8	136.4	253.9	335.3	323.0	227.2	264.2	433.3	195.3
1982	161.1	200.1	263.1	333.3	143.4	249.4	353.9	313.6	235.3	263.2	455.5	193.5
1983	229.5	259.9	226.9	235.1	92.1	201.8	318.3	284.2	202.6	230.1	562.9	120.0
1984	226.1	261.9	233.9	265.8	133.1	306.0	308.1	310.0	190.2	280.5	585.6	116.6
1985	218.9	269.8	222.3	243.2	159.1	184.4	292.6	290.9	183.3	276.0	565.4	129.2
1986	218.2	231.1	214.6	240.9	145.5	228.5	288.1	282.6	148.9	288.5	533.7	184.5
1987	178.2	177.6	192.2	251.9	131.0	213.8	264.5	262.6	138.3	222.1	519.1	298.0
1988	168.6	196.4	167.5	232.8	99.0	213.8	282.0	257.6	177.6	248.0	540.6	265.4
1989	158.4	207.0	142.9	192.9	79.9	161.3	218.9	189.8	141.1	201.4	484.9	422.9
1990	153.6	165.2	176.9	193.4	88.7	157.5	213.3	221.4	140.1	218.2	481.9	398.5
1991	157.7	212.8	199.2	180.9	95.8	198.1	200.6	224.4	142.3	226.4	459.9	498.9
1992	148.6	134.1	219.5	191.9	86.2	213.3	163.7	205.0	118.7	221.6	372.3	566.0
1993	129.3	147.7	187.0	211.1	76.9	174.0	160.5	187.3	110.8	206.7	296.6	676.1
1994	118.4	142.8	177.6	185.9	78.2	205.7	141.8	169.6	107.3	189.5	252.2	750.5
1995	118.5	139.2	153.3	140.2	60.5	228.0	117.3	187.8	114.3	270.5	219.0	699.4
1996	106.3	138.1	159.2	139.7	69.5	177.5	118.7	167.5	102.8	256.2	194.1	761.5

	F	AW	HP	LP	EM	OAW	NM		MS	SS	US	UNS
1997	114.5	135.0	116.9	108.5	37.6	91.5	212.6	-	117.8	109.1	175.1	702.9
1998	120.0	128.4	141.8	128.8	57.9	127.5	215.9	-	104.7	114.0	207.2	646.5
1999	110.3	121.9	123.1	119.2	47.5	140.8	164.0	-	100.5	82.6	190.9	791.2
2000	85.4	69.5	113.2	191.5	65.2	16.7	129.6	-	136.5	89.5	215.1	845.1
2001	75.4	55.0	125.0	174.6	57.9	46.8	148.7	-	155.7	137.4	203.2	774.7
2002	103.4	121.2	138.7	141.9	46.8	37.6	150.1	-	223.5	139.9	264.8	403.4

F=Farmers OA=Other Agricultural Workers HP=Higher Professional LP=Lower Professional EM=Employers & Managers SE=Salaried Employees INM=Intermediate Non-Manual ONM=Other Non-Manual SM=Skilled Manual SS=Semi-Skilled US=Unskilled UNS=Unspecified AW=Agricultural Workers OAW=Own Account Workers NM=Non-manual MS=Manual Skilled

Table 3.14a First admissions by diagnosis 1965–2002. Rates per 100,000 total population.

	Organic psychoses	Schizophrenia	Affective disorders	Neuroses	Personality disorders	Alcoholic disorders	Drug dependence	Mental handicap	Unspecified
1965	32.5	51.5	-	46.5	2.7	24.2	1.4	9.2	0.9
1966	34.6	53.7	-	54.2	3.2	27.7	0.9	7.9	0.4
1967	35.2	52.6	-	56.7	3.7	30.0	1.2	9.3	0.4
1968	36.8	51.6	-	59.2	3.4	37.5	1.7	9.1	5.9
1969	36.5	52.8	-	64.5	4.5	41.1	2.3	8.4	3.1
1970	35.4	53.3	-	67.0	4.4	43.4	2.5	8.3	3.8
1971	27.0	72.0	68.8	43.5	11.4	53.3	2.6	9.5	5.6
1972	31.5	75.9	80.9	41.7	14.7	58.8	2.6	8.8	5.5
1973	29.0	78.4	82.5	43.4	13.9	69.2	3.5	8.7	7.3
1974	26.8	73.5	87.5	39.4	13.1	69.5	2.2	7.4	7.0
1975	25.2	70.5	81.6	39.7	14.3	73.8	2.7	7.4	6.3
1976	25.0	68.9	81.3	42.2	15.0	74.0	2.5	7.1	7.5
1977	23.1	64.5	76.8	37.2	13.4	84.5	2.4	6.1	6.9
1978	22.1	62.8	77.3	42.1	13.5	85.2	2.3	4.9	6.0
1979	20.8	57.7	65.7	35.1	10.5	74.6	1.5	5.0	6.5
1980	23.1	56.5	44.1	33.0	9.6	73.6	1.6	3.1	6.1
1981	19.2	42.1	77.2	18.2	11.0	74.2	3.2	3.4	2.9
1982	17.9	39.9	85.2	20.6	11.8	74.7	3.1	3.0	1.8
1983	18.9	36.9	83.3	16.8	11.1	68.2	3.6	3.1	2.1
1984	16.2	37.0	90.0	17.9	12.4	71.9	2.9	3.5	1.9
1985	17.9	32.9	89.5	15.9	12.1	69.4	2.7	2.7	1.6
1986	17.3	31.5	87.3	13.6	10.3	65.4	3.3	2.7	7.9
1987	13.9	31.7	81.2	16.3	9.4	61.7	2.9	2.6	10.4
1988	11.9	35.2	83.1	14.1	9.4	65.0	2.9	3.0	9.7
1989	11.2	31.4	71.7	15.5	10.4	63.1	2.1	2.0	5.3
1990	10.9	31.1	77.8	15.7	10.4	60.6	3.0	2.5	2.1
1991	10.7	34.9	78.9	17.4	10.0	63.3	3.5	1.9	4.0
1992	10.5	32.3	75.8	15.4	9.8	55.3	4.1	2.3	4.7
1993	8.7	28.4	82.1	16.2	10.6	49.2	4.7	2.3	4.2
1994	10.3	27.1	73.3	18.6	11.4	48.2	5.6	2.5	4.4
1995	9.8	30.2	76.8	19.8	9.5	45.0	7.5	2.4	4.5
1996	9.9	30.7	71.9	19.1	11.4	45.7	6.7	2.8	5.9
1997	10.4	27.5	68.7	18.9	9.7	40.6	6.5	2.5	9.5
1998	9.8	25.3	76.7	20.5	7.5	43.8	7.2	1.6	4.4
1999	8.1	27.2	77.9	19.2	8.2	41.7	7.9	1.4	5.6
2000	8.8	29.9	84.9	17.0	7.2	41.0	7.8	1.5	4.2
2001	6.7	31.9	86.1	16.5	7.1	39.9	8.4	1.2	4.8
2002	5.8	23.2	83.0	15.0	5.8	36.1	6.3	1.0	5.3

Table 3.15a First admission rates for schizophrenia, affective disorders and alcoholic disorders 1965–2002. Rates per 100,000 total population.

	Schizophrenia		Affective disorders		Alcoholic disorders	
	Male	Female	Male	Female	Male	Female
1965	58.7	44.2	–	–	42.2	6.1
1966	63.0	44.4	–	–	46.3	9.0
1967	64.0	41.2	–	–	49.1	10.6
1968	67.1	42.6	–	–	65.1	9.5
1969	60.4	44.3	–	–	69.4	12.0
1970	62.5	43.4	–	–	73.7	12.5
1971	74.7	69.3	52.3	85.5	87.9	18.3
1972	74.3	77.6	62.5	99.4	99.7	17.4
1973	79.4	77.4	64.5	100.7	113.7	24.2
1974	73.4	73.7	68.7	106.6	115.5	23.0
1975	74.5	66.4	60.7	102.7	119.6	27.5
1976	68.2	69.7	59.6	103.1	120.1	27.5
1977	65.5	63.5	57.3	96.5	137.7	30.8
1978	62.3	63.3	59.9	94.9	140.3	29.5
1979	61.8	53.5	54.0	77.6	120.8	27.8
1980	61.3	51.6	34.3	54.0	115.8	30.9
1981	49.8	34.2	60.6	94.0	118.7	29.3
1982	44.7	35.0	65.4	105.1	120.2	28.7
1983	43.7	30.0	65.3	101.5	111.0	24.9
1984	41.4	32.6	69.1	111.1	115.4	28.0
1985	39.4	26.3	76.0	103.1	111.1	27.4
1986	38.3	24.7	74.5	100.2	104.2	26.1
1987	36.3	27.0	71.5	91.1	96.5	26.7
1988	40.9	29.4	71.2	95.0	100.2	29.5
1989	36.4	26.4	62.2	81.1	96.5	29.7
1990	37.2	25.0	67.2	88.4	93.5	27.7
1991	41.7	28.2	67.8	90.0	98.5	28.1
1992	36.7	28.0	64.6	87.1	86.7	23.8
1993	33.4	23.5	72.6	91.5	73.7	24.7
1994	31.9	22.4	65.9	80.6	74.1	22.3
1995	36.4	24.1	71.0	82.5	65.7	24.4
1996	35.2	26.2	64.4	79.3	67.6	24.0
1997	34.1	21.0	63.4	74.0	60.5	20.9
1998	31.7	19.1	72.2	81.2	65.2	22.7
1999	34.1	20.4	75.0	80.7	61.3	22.3
2000	36.4	23.6	80.4	89.3	60.9	21.4
2001	39.3	24.6	81.9	90.2	58.0	22.0
2002	29.7	16.8	79.6	86.3	49.4	23.0

Table 3.16a Non-voluntary first admissions 1971–2002. Percentages with rates per 100,000 total population.

	Percentage			Rate		
	Male	Female	Total	Male	Female	Total
1971	21.2	19.5	20.4	62.9	51.2	57.1
1972	21.3	18.7	20.1	67.6	52.0	59.8
1973	21.0	16.8	19.1	70.7	48.6	59.7
1974	19.6	18.5	19.1	65.6	52.4	59.0
1975	19.7	17.5	18.7	63.3	47.8	55.6
1976	20.7	16.7	18.8	66.3	46.6	56.5
1977	19.7	17.1	18.5	63.7	45.5	54.6
1978	18.7	16.0	17.5	60.8	41.2	51.0
1979	17.0	15.1	16.2	49.5	33.3	41.4
1980	15.9	15.3	15.6	44.5	34.0	39.3
1981	17.0	14.5	15.9	48.4	31.8	40.1
1982	-	-	-	-	-	-
1983	16.8	14.5	15.8	45.9	31.2	38.6
1984	15.5	15.1	15.3	43.6	34.3	39.0
1985	16.5	15.5	16.1	46.0	32.7	39.4
1986	16.5	15.3	16.0	44.7	31.9	38.3
1987	16.3	13.9	15.3	42.0	27.8	34.9
1988	-	-	-	-	-	-
1989	16.1	15.3	15.8	38.8	28.2	33.5
1990	14.6	11.6	13.3	35.3	21.5	28.4
1991	15.1	13.4	14.3	38.9	25.5	32.2
1992	13.3	10.8	12.2	31.5	19.9	25.7
1993	13.7	11.6	12.7	31.2	21.5	26.3
1994	14.3	12.5	13.5	32.8	21.7	27.3
1995	16.0	11.1	13.8	36.8	20.0	28.4
1996	16.3	12.0	14.4	36.6	22.1	29.3
1997	15.3	11.8	13.8	34.0	19.6	26.8
1998	13.4	10.8	12.3	30.2	18.3	24.2
1999	15.8	11.9	14.1	35.7	20.1	27.9
2000	14.0	11.6	13.0	32.1	20.5	26.3
2001	13.1	10.7	12.0	29.8	19.0	24.4
2002	14.6	12.1	13.5	29.3	19.6	24.5

Table 3.17a First admissions by health board area 1972–2002. Rates per 100,000 total population.

	EHB/EHRA	MHB	MWHB	NEHB	NWHB	SEHB	SHB	WHB
1972	327.7	278.3	304.3	240.9	223.2	335.4	295.4	244.5
1973	339.1	236.8	338.3	238.3	222.7	331.0	315.3	304.5
1974	302.8	223.0	340.6	245.1	227.8	320.7	319.9	303.5
1975	298.0	243.7	378.0	259.4	237.9	335.3	298.5	259.3
1976	294.0	293.4	341.7	219.5	280.7	310.4	306.4	318.9
1977	300.1	264.3	336.9	253.3	279.1	322.8	295.0	246.5
1978	301.2	278.3	292.9	261.8	255.6	331.0	304.7	218.4
1979	251.5	260.1	270.2	214.9	247.5	309.1	227.8	258.0
1980	236.8	252.5	271.6	206.4	264.1	299.3	223.2	271.6
1981	241.1	254.1	305.1	191.4	250.9	280.5	247.4	245.2
1982	238.1	283.9	320.8	192.5	240.2	296.6	254.2	263.9
1983	231.2	257.2	280.6	191.3	233.9	280.8	237.6	259.5
1984	231.1	255.2	264.7	190.3	233.4	269.1	313.5	263.3
1985	240.7	239.9	295.5	172.3	203.6	274.4	233.6	268.0
1986	243.4	211.7	265.0	183.4	199.3	264.2	227.7	266.8
1987	255.4	202.3	254.0	175.0	188.7	236.2	193.2	237.8
1988	260.5	193.9	292.9	190.6	175.7	219.9	204.0	236.4
1989	230.3	195.2	250.4	160.9	184.3	212.0	186.4	214.5
1990	228.7	166.4	251.4	185.1	200.7	221.6	184.0	205.0
1991	227.2	181.3	228.3	198.7	213.4	223.9	241.9	219.0
1992	225.9	184.1	183.9	155.9	188.0	207.8	199.5	259.5
1993	223.6	174.0	172.1	179.4	194.1	196.1	182.7	258.4
1994	219.8	180.3	169.0	172.8	176.3	192.5	183.3	236.0
1995	217.9	205.9	182.2	169.6	183.0	199.9	195.4	224.2
1996	218.3	189.7	197.3	157.6	179.7	227.0	176.8	219.3
1997	206.5	196.1	169.4	146.0	193.0	192.6	181.8	215.7
1998	209.6	187.8	194.9	137.5	175.9	203.1	187.1	206.9
1999	212.5	206.3	163.4	137.8	173.1	216.8	170.7	228.2
2000	198.9	210.2	164.3	150.3	177.8	164.8	322.8	200.7
2001	223.2	224.3	144.8	116.6	207.7	145.3	282.2	211.7
2002	175.6	202.3	147.2	122.3	165.6	206.1	198.7	214.8